T0285788

IMAGES
of America

HISTORIC HOUSES OF THE CONNECTICUT RIVER VALLEY

Especially after the Civil War, the scenic beauty of the Connecticut River Valley attracted tourists to its peaceful colonial villages and its mountain summit hotels, which offered dramatic bird's-eye views of the river towns in their natural settings. In this c. 1865 carte de visite souvenir photograph, boarders at the Mountain House stand atop Table Rock on Sugar Loaf Mountain in South Deerfield, Massachusetts. From the precipitous cliff, they enjoyed the panoramic view across the river, with farmsteads below, the houses of Sunderland across the river, and Mount Toby in the distance. (University of Massachusetts Amherst Libraries, Special Collections and University Archives, W.E.B. Du Bois Library.)

ON THE COVER: Oscar and Julia Hedström, seen here around 1915, enjoyed watching Main Street parades from their circular pergola in front of their home in Portland, Connecticut. Racing bicyclist Oscar Hedström developed a prototype of the modern motorcycle in a shop across the Connecticut River in Middletown. Partnering with fellow champion bicyclist George Hendee upriver in Springfield, Massachusetts, they founded the Indian Motocycle Company. Hedström, a brilliant mechanical engineer, is considered by many to be the father of American motorcycle design. (Susan Alyson Young and Charles Young Collection.)

IMAGES
of America

HISTORIC HOUSES OF THE CONNECTICUT RIVER VALLEY

Alain Munkittrick

ARCADIA
PUBLISHING

Copyright © 2023 by Alain Munkittrick
ISBN 978-1-4671-0833-1

Published by Arcadia Publishing
Charleston, South Carolina

Printed in the United States of America

Library of Congress Control Number: 2022950452

For all general information, please contact Arcadia Publishing:
Telephone 843-853-2070
Fax 843-853-0044
E-mail sales@arcadiapublishing.com
For customer service and orders:
Toll-Free 1-888-313-2665

Visit us on the Internet at www.arcadiapublishing.com

This book is dedicated to the memory of Connecticut River photographers who documented life in the valley, capturing its history and charm, including George Bradford Brainerd (1845–1887) of Haddam, Connecticut, Clifton Johnson (1865–1940) of Hadley, Massachusetts, and Paesiello Emerson (1832–1927) of Longmeadow, Massachusetts.

CONTENTS

ACKNOWLEDGMENTS

This search for historic houses would have been impossible without the guidance of many historical society volunteers, knowledgeable librarians, museum curators, archivists, and local history buffs. Aside from the many people associated with the institutions named in these acknowledgements, I wish to thank the following individuals who also provided me with sage advice, promising leads, photographs, and research assistance: Maggie and Sue Arnold, Amy Barron-Burke, Mary Biddle (Smith College Library), Carol Boynton (Orford Free Library), David R. Cecchi, Devin Colman, Hannah Criser, Diana Hunt Edgerton, Margaret McCutcheon Faber, Erin Farley and Jocelyn Weaver (Connecticut Landmarks), Paula Graves (Orford Historical Society), Wick Griswold, Judy Hayward (Historic Windsor Inc.), Maureen Heher (Hartford History Center), William Hosley, Susan Lisk (Porter Phelps Huntington Museum), Amy Kilkenny (Wadsworth Atheneum Library & Archives), Samantha Lee (Enfield Library), Dione Longley, Jane Louis (Oliver Ellsworth Homestead), Robert McDougall (Portland Historical Society), Wayne McElreavy (Claremont Historical Society), Tracey McFadden (Friends of the Morrill Homestead), Charity Appell McNabb, Elizabeth Merriam, Isolde Motley, Susan Motycka, Tina Panik (Avon Library), Karen Parsons (Loomis Chaffee School), Geoffrey Paul, Tom Piezzo, Sarah Rooker (Norwich Historical Society), Isabelle Seggerman, Ken Slater (Stellafane), Peter and Susan Smith, Walter Spilsbury, Susan Waide, Carolyn Wakeman, Vi and Mike Welker (Windsor Vermont Historical Association), Adele West-Fisher (St. Johnsbury Athenaeum), Terri Wilson (Avon Historical Society), and Willis Wood.

I wish to especially thank Denise Desplaines who assisted me with photographic layouts and Rosemary Munkittrick with editing. Jeff Ruetsche, Angel Prohaska, and Stacia Bannerman at Arcadia Publishing deftly shepherded this project through to its completion.

I am grateful to the many people up and down the Connecticut River Valley who assisted me with this book, leading me to important houses, local contacts, and wonderful stories, patiently answering my questions, and providing scanned images from their archives and personal collections. These people are listed below in connection with the abbreviations used in the text. The photographs in this book are courtesy of these organizations and generous individuals.

AM	Alain Munkittrick Collection
BFA/WF	Billings Family Archives, the Woodstock Foundation Inc., Woodstock, Vermont, Marianne C. Zephir
BHS	Brattleboro Historical Society, Carol Farrington, Bill Holiday
BM/BPL, BC	Brooklyn Museum/Brooklyn Public Library, Brooklyn Collection
BRB&ML	Yale Collection of American Literature, Beinecke Rare Book and Manuscript Library, Yale University, June Can
BradHS	Bradford Historical Society, Meroa Benjamin
CHS	Charlestown Historical Society; Lynne Fisk, Marge Reed
ChHS	Chester Historical Society; Diane Lindsay, Marta Daniels
CSHC	Communal Societies Collection, Hamilton College, Christian Goodwillie
CTHS	The Connecticut Historical Society, Sierra Dixon, Tasha Caswell
CTSL	Connecticut State Library, Maria Paxi, Lizette Pelletier
DCL/RSC	Dartmouth College Library, Rauner Special Collections, Scout Noffke
EHHS	East Haddam Historical Society, Marianne Halpin, Joyce Maynard
EnHS	Enfield Historical Society, Michael Miller
EsHS	Essex Historical Society, Melissa Josefiak
FLib	Forbes Library, Northampton, Massachusetts, Dylan Gaffney
FLib/CCPL&M	Forbes Library, Northampton, Massachusetts, Calvin Coolidge Presidential Library & Museum, Julie Bartlett Nelson

FMtToR	Fruitlands Museum, the Trustees of Reservations, Anna M. Thompson
FoFAH	Friends of the Farm at Hilltop, administrator to the estate of June Hale Cook © 2007, Ray Pioggia, Tony Peterson
FoHT	Friends of Heublein Tower; Jay T. Willerup
GCSPA	Gillette Castle State Park Archives, Paul Schiller
GWVS	George Walter Vincent Smith Art Museum, Stephen Sullivan
HaHS	Haddam Historical Society, Elizabeth Malloy
HBSC	Harriet Beecher Stowe Center, Elizabeth G. Burgess
HN	Historic Northampton, Marie Panik, M.J. Maaccardini
HNE	Historic New England, Donna E. Russo
HPL/HHR	The Holyoke History Room, Holyoke Public Library, Eileen Crosby
HPL/VSDC	From the Vincent S. D'Addario Collection, The Holyoke History Room, Holyoke Public Library
HSG	The Historical Society of Glastonbury, Phyllis Reed
HtHS	Hartland Historical Society, Pip Parker
JLib	The Jones Library Inc., Amherst, Massachusetts, Jennifer L. Bauman, Katherine Whitcomb
JBColl	John Bolles III Collection
KML	Kent Memorial Library, Suffield History Room, Anne Borg, Art Sikes, Laurie Tavino, Wendy Taylor
LHS	Lebanon Historical Society, Nicole Ford Burley
LHSA@FGM	Lyme Historical Society Archives at the Florence Griswold Museum, Mell Scalzi
LOC	Library of Congress Prints and Photographs Collection
LPC/BPL	Boston Public Library, Leslie Jones Collection, Bob Collum, on behalf of the family of Leslie R. Jones
LPH&LHA	Lyme Public Hall & Local History Archives, Julie Hughes
LTUSA	The Landmark Trust USA, Susan McMahon and University of Vermont Silver Special Collections Library, Chris Burns
MCHS	Middlesex County Historical Society, Jesse Nasta, Deborah Shapiro
MHCA&SC	Mount Holyoke College Archives & Special Collections, Deborah Richards, Micha Broadnax
MHL	Middle Haddam Library, Janet McDonald, Linda Rincks
NARA	National Archives and Records Administration
NGA	National Gallery of Art, Peter Huestis
NMHA	Northfield Mount Hermon Archives, Peter Weis
NPG	National Portrait Gallery
OCHS	Ontario County Historical Society, Cody Grabhorn
OSHS	Old Saybrook Historical Society, Theodora Kopcha, Marie Mcfarlin
PTP	Prudence Taylor & T.J. Palmer Collection, Cathy J. Reed
RPC	Ray Pioggia Collection
SAAM	Smithsonian American Art Museum
SAHS	Springfield Art and Historical Society, Vermont; Hugh and Roseanne Putnam
SANHSA	Springfield Armory NHS Archives, Alex MacKenzie
SAY&CY	Susan Alyson Young and Charles Young Collection
SCUA/UMAL	Porter-Phelps-Huntington Family Papers, Robert S. Cox Special Collections and University Archives Research Center, University of Massachusetts Amherst Libraries, Annie Sollinger
SLHRI	Schlesinger Library, Harvard Radcliffe Institute, Laura Peimer
SSC	Susan Smith Collection
TRF	The Rockfall Foundation, Tony Marino
TWMLH	The Wadsworth Mansion at Long Hill, Joyce Kirkpatrick, Catie Griffin, Jessica Hess

UMAL	University of Massachusetts Amherst Libraries, Special Collections and University Archives, W.E.B. Du Bois Library, Anne Moore and Annie Sollinger
VDHP	Vermont Division for Historic Preservation, Laura Trieschmann
VHS	Vermont Historical Society, Paul Carnahan, Kate Phillips, Marjorie Strong
WaHS	Walpole Historical Society, William Rauner
WAMofAA	Wadsworth Atheneum Museum of Art Archives, Hartford, Connecticut, Stacey Stachow
WDSM	Webb-Deane-Stevens Museum, Richard Malley
WeHS	Wethersfield Historical Society, Gillie Johnson, Kristina Oschmann
WiHS	Windsor Historical Society, Windsor, Connecticut, Michelle Tom
WMA	Wistariahurst Museum Archives, Holyoke, Massachusetts, Penni Martorell
WmHS	Williamsburg Historical Society, Eric Weber
WMSH	The Lyman & Merrie Wood Museum of Springfield History, Margaret Humberston, Cliff McCarthy
WVtHS	Weathersfield Vermont Historical Society, Ellen Clattenburg, Patti Arrison
YUAG	Yale University Art Gallery

It would be impossible to include all of the most important houses of the Connecticut River Valley within these thematically arranged chapters. Those selected include well-known designated national historic landmarks, houses that have regional significance, and others that have escaped attention until now. In all cases, I have selected these for their architectural significance and/or their historical associations.

INTRODUCTION

New England's Connecticut River is the flowing artery at the center of a wide valley that extends over 400 miles north to south from the Canadian border to Long Island Sound. It is the longest river in New England. The river's course defines the border between Vermont and New Hampshire, creating what has come to be considered the upper valley. Heading south, it bisects Massachusetts and Connecticut, forming the lower valley region. Its extensive watershed encompasses much of New England. The river is fed by many tributaries and smaller streams that flow down from rocky hills. About 10,000 years ago, when the Wisconsin Glacier retreated northward, its meltwaters left behind a wide lake about 140 miles long, which was dammed near present-day central Connecticut. This Lake Hitchcock, as named by geologists, eventually drained and the Connecticut River's meandering course remained. This course has shifted over time due to the earth's settling, as well as from sedimentary deposits that have washed down from upriver and from its eroding banks.

Indigenous people who farmed, fished, and hunted along the Connecticut River Valley for thousands of years called the river *quinetucket*, or variations on this. Roughly translated as "along the long tidal river," the name reflected the effects of Long Island Sound's tides on the ebb and flow of the river in the lower valley. The natives' earliest shelters were dug into the sides of the riverbank. Later abodes, moved to higher ground, were fashioned from tree branches, bark, and grass coverings. These people navigated the river in boats dug out of tree trunks, later crafting more lightweight canoes of bark on wood frames. Their boatbuilding ingenuity facilitated trade with tribal communities surprisingly remote from the Connecticut River Valley. We have come to understand that this indigenous society was more sophisticated than European settlers condescendingly characterized it as. Other than important archaeological sites, however, few known physical remnants of these native settlements remain.

Europeans arrived in the early 1600s. They originally came to the Connecticut River Valley to barter with indigenous natives for beaver and other pelts, which were highly valued in Europe. These traders created riverside outposts and amassed land holdings along the lower river valley, often taking advantage of the native population by trade, guile, or force. Violent conflicts resulted. After these fur traders mapped the inland waterway, settlers from New England's east coast Bay Colony and Long Island Sound's villages relocated to the valley. They usually came to farm the rich alluvial soils deposited along its banks, as well as along the banks of its 38 main tributaries, including the Hockanum, Farmington, and Scantic Rivers in Connecticut; the Westfield, Chicopee, Deerfield, Green, and Millers Rivers in Massachusetts; the Ashuelot and Sugar Rivers in New Hampshire, and the Williams and Black Rivers of Vermont. These settlers came to call the Connecticut, into which all others flowed, "the Great River."

During the late 18th century, European settlements expanded east and west into the uplands where the tributaries and streams could be redirected and harnessed to turn wheels at gristmills and sawmills. When dammed for timed releases, the falls would also power machines in small mills to manufacture a variety of goods. Before turnpikes, canals, and railroads were constructed in the 19th century, the river was New England's superhighway, uniting diverse communities in a cultural subregion well into the 1800s. Those who controlled transportation on the river became wealthy from shipbuilding and its related industries, the operation of ferries and toll bridges, and investments in downriver, coastal, and international trade, with its many risks and rewards. The men who profited from these endeavors headed important, interrelated families. They quickly came to dominate the legal, political, and religious affairs of their communities. Reflecting their power and authority, they were later known as the "River Gods" (chapter one).

Until well into the 19th century, most valley families farmed for themselves, often bartering with their neighbors for other necessary goods and services. Some of these families acquired, by purchase or marriage, significantly large acreage, which required tenant contract labor, paid labor (often indentured), or unpaid (slave) labor. Many farmers raised livestock and harvested lumber and agricultural produce, which was shipped, early on, to supply the West Indies plantations of the Caribbean Sea. These "River Producers" (chapter two) amassed extensive farmsteads that often passed down in the same family for generations. Throughout the Connecticut River Valley, the dwellings and barns of these farmsteads were frequently built with great sophistication, reflecting their owners' wealth and gentility.

Connecticut "River Patriots and Pols" (chapter three) are readily identifiable from all periods of American history. They crafted and amended constitutions, served in local, state, and national legislatures, and sat in judgment at court. They served, returned wounded, or died in all of America's wars. Many of the homes associated with these patriots and politicians are shrines to their legacy and sacrifice. Some are national landmarks visited annually by many.

The ingenuity of Connecticut River Valley people, coupled with capital investments earned from farming and trading, plus bountiful natural resources, especially abundant waterpower, gave rise to the "River Makers" (chapter four). These capitalists and industrialists manufactured a wide range of products for local, regional, national, and sometimes international markets. Entrepreneurial men and women shipped their goods on the river on specially designed rafts, flat-bottomed boats or barges, sailing sloops and schooners, and steamboats. Subsequently, with the construction of turnpike roads, hand-dug canals, and railroads, valley manufacturers expanded trade more efficiently with the Boston, New York, and Midwestern markets, earning them enormous profits. However, steam technology and cheaper labor found elsewhere would eventually spell the demise of most of these industries.

Nonetheless, by the latter half of the 19th century, enduring family wealth and more leisure time resulted in a new lifestyle enjoyed by the more fortunate Connecticut "River Gentry" (chapter five). Influenced by fashionable European trends and fashions, families created lavish suburban villas set in lushly designed landscapes. Many established gentleman farms, exhibiting the most modern agricultural techniques. A few constructed grand, landscaped estates with panoramic views of the river valley and mountains beyond. The picturesque and scenic Connecticut River Valley attracted steamboat tourists and later automobile motorists to its quaint colonial villages of white clapboard homes with green or black shutters and fenced gardens facing gentrified town greens. Many seasonal visitors, so charmed, stayed and built summer places and permanent homes.

The Connecticut River Valley's diverse natural beauty was also sought after for the home sites of important artists, writers, actors, and other "River Masters" of their crafts (chapter six). They brought new energy to sleepy towns and urban vitality to aging cities. Private schools, religious seminaries, and respected colleges and universities that reflected the intellectual ferment of the valley also attracted teachers, researchers, and students from far afield. In many cases, modern ideas that they brought with them variously delighted and appalled plainspoken locals set in their ways and traditions. But the overriding, innate characteristics of the homegrown Connecticut River Valley Yankee—ingenuity, tenacity, and fair-mindedness—created generations of well-educated men and women eager to change the world around them. The homes of these "River Reformers" (chapter seven) introduce us to the stories of their idealism.

The Connecticut River's geography, ecology, seasonal transformations, and course changes over the years had profound effects on the lives of those who chose to live along its banks. Indigenous communities managed to live here for thousands of years, generally in harmony with its rhythms and changes. Europeans, with their individualistic mindsets, altered the valley within decades of inhabiting its watershed. The producers and the makers left their imprints in many subtle and not-so-subtle ways. Intervales were drained and plowed, streams diverted, canals and locks erected, dams and bridges built, and sewage and manufacturing wastes dumped. They changed the river. The lives of those who lived along the river's shores had a profound effect on American history in ways that this book can only touch on. Their homes, constructed over the course of a mere 300 years, are one important manifestation of this imprint. They remain tangible and, hopefully, lasting legacies of the Connecticut River Valley's fascinating history.

One

River Gods

While the original dwellings of European immigrants were rudimentary, during the second half of the 18th century, the elite class of the river valley constructed mansions reflecting their wealth and status. These homes, often constructed and serviced by indentured or enslaved people, were the homesteads of county magistrates, religious leaders, and military officers. Early accounts referred to these families as "mansion people" or "river gods." Their Georgian-style homes were pretentiously scaled, had spacious, center stair halls that impressed, and elegant parlors enhanced with expensive paneling and painted decorations. Expansive double-pitched (gambrel) roofs imitated government buildings. Rare, painted clapboard siding, framed with pilasters and corner quoining; classical window surrounds; and most importantly, broken scroll or triangular pedimented main entrances serving as frontispieces around wide double doors—these are the hallmarks of the Connecticut River Valley style. Stylistically outdated by the end of the century (and, after the Revolutionary War, often associated with Tory sympathizers), the new gentry of the valley turned to other architectural models for inspiration. Federal and Greek Revival styles proliferated.

By the mid-19th century, turnpikes and canals bypassed the Connecticut River's rapids, and with the development of steam-powered and flat-bottomed boats, the river was navigable to upper valley towns. Traders north of the major settlement at Springfield, Massachusetts, controlled river transportation. They partnered with warehouse and store owners in the lower valley to market or trade livestock, lumber, and agricultural produce. Hartford and Middletown in Connecticut became viable inland seaports, extending the valley traders' reach to American coastal ports, the West Indies, Europe, and the Far East. Rum, molasses, rice, tobacco, tea, dry goods, and enslaved people were shipped north in exchange. Shipbuilding to service this trade became the valley's most important industry.

Wealth and political power came from investments in ships, stores, warehouses, wharves, rope and sail-making, chandlery, marine insurance, commission businesses, and investment banking. Families who also controlled cross-river ferries and bridges (earning valuable state charters) collected tolls and compounded their wealth with taverns and hotels, which flourished when tourists came to the valley in steamboats after 1850.

In 1836, John Warner Barber rendered the then 200-year-old Thomas Hooker House at Hartford, Connecticut, (above left). Hooker, a leading Puritan theologian, inspired the Fundamental Orders of 1639, the first written constitution. The ancient house was replicated on the state capitol grounds for Connecticut's tercentenary celebration in 1935 (above right). John Pynchon's c. 1661 house (below right) in the earliest settlement at Springfield, Massachusetts, was the grandest outside Boston. The brick garrison house served as a refuge for settlers during the siege of the town by native Americans during King Phillip's War in 1675, and became known as the Old Fort. Pynchon, a successful trader and owner of extensive properties along the river, was the son of the settlement's founder, William Pynchon, who had sailed up the Connecticut River and established a trading *entrepôt* there. Hartford artist Louis Ore etched William Pynchon's likeness (below left) in 1927. Both houses were typical First-Period types, derived from English building traditions with post-and-beam frames, central chimneys, steep roofs, overhanging stories, and small, leaded glass windows. (Above left, CTHS; above right, CTSL. Below left, David R. Cecchi Collection; below right, AM.)

The manse above (a term designated for important church parsonages of the river valley) was built for minister Ebenezer Gay in 1742 on Suffield, Connecticut's Main Street. It is one of the valley's earliest surviving houses with a gambrel roof and broken scroll pediment above its entrance. The Manse in Northampton, Massachusetts, is associated with the prominent theocratic Stoddard family. In 1685, Rev. Solomon Stoddard, the controversial "pope" of the river valley, built an older house here where his grandson theologian Jonathan Edwards lived briefly. The ell (1744) was originally the home of Col. John Stoddard, an influential civic leader. The 1782 house, with a gambrel roof, was built to the front of it by Solomon Stoddard, high sheriff of Hampshire County. Stoddard was forcibly removed from this house by a mob until he pledged to support the Continental Congress. (Above, KML; below, HN.)

The right wing of the Deacon John Loomis Homestead in Windsor, Connecticut, one of the earliest residences in the river valley was built by Joseph Loomis, an English woolen draper, after 1640. The five-bay portion was constructed by his son Deacon John Loomis in about 1688 (left). Loomis families lived here for 300 years until it was occupied by The Loomis School in 1944. Below is the house of Samuel Porter III (built in 1713) facing the green in Hadley, Massachusetts. Porter men, successfully engaging in farming and river trade, dominated the 18th-century economics and politics of western Massachusetts. Samuel's son Eleazer Porter enhanced the house in 1761 with a new entrance featuring a fashionable broken scroll pediment. (Left, photograph by Ezra Stoller, from the collection of the Loomis Chaffee Archives, Loomis Chaffee School; below, FLib.)

Judge Seth Wetmore's mansion (above) in Middletown, Connecticut, likely introduced Georgian high-style architecture to the lower river valley when built in 1744. Wetmore was an influential town magistrate and county court judge. Much of Oak Hill, as it was known, remains original. A notable exception is the fancy northeast parlor, removed in 1986 as a period room at Hartford's Wadsworth Atheneum. Notables including Jonathan Edwards (Wetmore's brother-in-law), Timothy Dwight IV, and Aaron Burr visited the Wetmores here on their extensive 1,000-acre farm overlooking the river valley. Enslaved people harvested crops for the Wetmores and dug the house's foundation. Mississippi-born George Washington gained his freedom during the Civil War and managed the Wetmore farm for over 60 years. He is seen at right with Wetmore descendant Elizabeth Wells in about 1899. (Above, MCHS; right, JBColl.)

River valley men of wealth or social standing often updated earlier houses with embellishments including the fashionable baroque doorways distinctive to the valley. In the 1750s, Parson Jonathan Ashley completely transformed an earlier center chimney house in Deerfield, Massachusetts, with a gambrel roof, center hall floor plan, interior paneling, and imported furnishings (above). Ashley House was moved twice and gutted for use as a tobacco warehouse in 1869, but was the first of 12 houses restored by the Flynt family as part of the Historic Deerfield project, opened to the public in 1948. Henry and Helen Flynt moved four houses to Deerfield, including the Josiah Dwight House (below) in 1950, which had been threatened by demolition in Springfield, Massachusetts. In 1754, Dwight remodeled the original 1725 David Ingersoll house, but the central chimney plan was retained. (Above, LOC; below, AM.)

An exceptional example of the Georgian style, with its original baroque Connecticut Valley doorway, was built by Ebenezer Grant in 1757–1758 in the East Windsor Hill section of South Windsor, Connecticut (above). While it was moved back from the highway in 1913, the house is generally as it was originally conceived. Grant was an early trader with the West Indies, exporting horses, barrel staves, and produce from local farms in exchange for rum and sugar. His trade with merchants in New York and Boston was reflected in the sophisticated design and furnishings of the house, a rarity for this period in the river valley. Another home with trendsetting interior decoration was that of the influential Rev. Eliphalet Williams, constructed by the townspeople of East Hartford, Connecticut, for him in 1751, and built by Benjamin Roberts (below). (Both, CTHS.)

Successful Connecticut River merchant Samuel "Marchant" Colton commissioned John Steele to build this grand Georgian-style home (1753–1755) in Longmeadow, Massachusetts (above). His store, which perhaps transacted more business than any other in western Massachusetts, was an unusual ell across the rear of the house (below). Colton owned enslaved Africans, a shipyard, and at least two ships that traded along the river, with the West Indies, and England. A Tory sympathizer, Colton's store was raided in 1776 by neighbors disguised as Native Americans, claiming he inflated prices for scarce merchandise, especially rum and salt. Although it was demolished in 1916, portions of the house live on. The stunning door went to the Boston Museum of Fine Arts, while other parts were repurposed for nearby homes. Longmeadow's Town Hall of 1930 was a replica of the lost house. (Both, LHS.)

In 1836, John Warner Barber wrote that this Georgian mansion (above) perched above the Connecticut River in East Haddam, Connecticut, "is distinguished for its bold and lofty terraces, and is a striking object to travelers passing on the river." Epaphroditus Champion, a merchant trader and important purchasing agent during the Revolutionary War, built it in 1794. The architect of this highly detailed house was William Sprats, a captured British soldier who stayed after the war to enjoy a career designing homes for Connecticut's elites. The estate, restored in 1940 by the painter Northam "Tod" Gould, came to be known as the Terraces for its stepped landscaping that led down to the river with walls retained by Haddam granite. The gambrel-roofed structure (below), now a home, is believed to have served originally as Epaphroditus's counting house at Champion's Landing. (Both, LOC.)

Epaphroditus Champion and his wife, Lucretia (Hubbard), painted in miniature on ivory in 1825 by Anson Dickinson, were typical of the Connecticut River Valley's mansion people who dominated river commerce in the 18th and early 19th centuries. Epaphroditus traded with the West Indies on his own ships and is remembered for driving a herd of cattle from Hartford to Washington's starving troops near Valley Forge. He served 10 years in the US Congress. (YUAG.)

About 1800, Thaddeus Leavitt Jr., a scion of a wealthy family, constructed this pretentious Federal-style home on Suffield, Connecticut's, Main Street. (The Italianate cupola was added later.) He and brother-in-law Luther Loomis were involved in lucrative trade with the West Indies. His daughter Jane married Jonathan Hunt Jr. of Brattleboro, Vermont, typical of familial relationships formed by commerce and social intercourse along the Connecticut River. (KML.)

By 1825, John and Sarah Holbrook of Brattleboro, Vermont (below), constructed this sophisticated Federal-style home (above). The house, built by Nathaniel Bliss, with its unique triple-peaked veranda supported by delicate Scamozzi colonettes, was a Brattleboro showpiece situated on 20 landscaped acres opposite the common. Deacon John Holbrook partnered with merchants in Hartford and New York to buy and sell products that he shipped along the Connecticut River in large, flat-bottomed boats. Holbrook pioneered this mode of transporting goods, which connected Vermont and New Hampshire producers with metropolitan markets, the Southern United States, and West Indies plantations. He retailed and wholesaled diverse products such as cotton, clothing, rum and sugar, ironware, fish and salted meats, tobacco, flax, rye, rice, flour, corn, and butter, and offered freighting service on his largest boats. (Above, BHS; below, AM.)

David Sumner was from Claremont, New Hampshire, but made his fortune in Hartland, Vermont, where he constructed this Federal-style brick mansion around 1811 (above), influenced by the work of architect Asher Benjamin in nearby Windsor. Sumner's business interests centered on the river and included cutting and shipping timber and milled lumber goods downriver, as well as the construction of roads, canals, locks, and toll bridges, and a ferry service across the river. He marketed his wood products in Springfield, Hartford, and Middletown, Connecticut. Francis Goodhue built an equally impressive home in Brattleboro, Vermont, in 1815 (below). Like Sumner, Goodhue had wide-ranging business interests that included sawmills and gristmills, wool carding and cotton spinning, distilling, farming, and real estate development. He was a booster of a canal project that would have linked Brattleboro with Northampton, Massachusetts. (Above, HtHS; below, AM.)

Bermudian ship captain Benjamin Williams erected his brick mansion (above) on a five-acre plot overlooking the Connecticut River in Middletown, Connecticut, around 1791. From here he oversaw his ships, trading goods and enslaved Africans with the West Indies. After 1797, his fortune was decimated by French privateers who seized many of his vessels. The brownstone quoining and dormers of this late Georgian house suggest Williams was influenced by high-style houses of Portsmouth and Newport, which Middletown rivaled in the 18th century. The house descended to Henry deKoven, a China trader. Built around 1784, only a few years before the Williams House, was the impressive mansion of Capt. Samuel Mather in Old Lyme, Connecticut (below). Mather owned West Indies trading ships, wharves, warehouses, and at least four enslaved Africans. (Above, TRF; below, AM.)

After moving to Old Lyme, Connecticut, in 1817, John Sill engaged the valley's master builder, Samuel Belcher, to design and construct this gracious Federal-style home in the Noyestown section (above in 1885). Sill, a merchant importer, but also a "customs runner," left debts behind, which by 1819 caught up with him. While his wife's Noyes family tried to bail him out, he was eventually jailed in New Haven. (LHSA@FGM.)

In 1842, Charles Chandler Griswold erected this Regency-style house on the foundation of his father, Deacon John Griswold's, home at Old Lyme, Connecticut's, Griswold Point overlooking the Connecticut River's confluence with Long Island Sound. The Black Hall district at Griswold Point was the family seat of the influential Griswold family of Connecticut governors and New York merchants in Old Lyme. Charles, a silent partner in his brother John's shipping business, planted the arch of elm trees that bordered the lane leading to the house. (LHSA@FGM.)

The original brick Federal period core of this house in Wethersfield, Connecticut, was likely built by postmaster Elisha Boardman before 1792. Capt. John Hurlbut purchased it in 1804. Hurlbut, a coastal trader, was the first mate on the ship *Neptune*, which had made a highly profitable three-year voyage to Canton, trading sealskins there for silk, porcelain, and tea—one of the earliest voyages to China of an American ship circumnavigating the world. In the 1860s, Levi Goodwin, who had mined and built roads and bridges in California during the 1849 gold rush, transformed it in the then-popular Italianate style, adding the projecting gable and entrance porch, bracketed roof topped by a cupola, and verandas. In 1908, newlyweds and new owners Jane and Howard Dunham (below) redecorated the interior parlors with ceiling frescoes and Rococo Revival wallpapers. (Both, WeHS.)

In 1819, Capt. Henry Champlin moved into his new home, the Federal-style core of this house at Essex, Connecticut. Four years earlier, Champlin married Amelia Prudence Hayden, who had inherited a small fortune from her grandfather Ebenezer Hayden, a wealthy Essex shipbuilder. Henry Champlin, a highly respected shipmaster, was commodore for the innovative Black X line that pioneered regularly scheduled packet sailing ships between New York and London. He, like other Connecticut River packet captains, bought shares in the ships they captained, parlaying great profits into real estate and loan investments in the lower valley. From the c. 1850 veranda with Egyptian Revival–style palm leaf columns and crenelated roof trimming, the family could enjoy the view over Essex's South Cove (below). (Above, EsHS; below, CTHS.)

Capt. Henry Hovey (above inset) was a mariner following in his brother-in-law Henry Champlin's footsteps, sailing ships between New York and London for the Black X line. In 1850, Hovey was an international hero after rescuing 180 passengers and crew of the sinking *Helena Sloman*. His costly Italianate home (above) in Essex, Connecticut, was built in 1857 by N. Jones Pratt and mason Ambrose Post, to the plans provided by New Haven architect Henry Austin. Hovey lost the house with the reversal of his fortunes after his ship *Amazon* was likely sunk by Confederate saboteurs near Portsmouth, England, in 1863. He died tragically, going down with the steamship *Lodona* off the Florida coast in 1871. Stripped of its ornamentation in 1922 and with a Neoclassical portico (below), the house later served as the Lord Essex Restaurant. (Both, EsHS.)

In 1697, the Warner family purchased the west bank of Selden's Twelve Mile Island Farm on the Connecticut River in Chester, Connecticut. Jonathan Warner bought out his siblings' interests and acquired the east bank through marriage to Elizabeth Selden. In 1769, he established a toll ferry, and together with his productive farm, fishing, and sailing ships that traded with coastal ports and the Caribbean, he became a wealthy man. (The Chester-Hadlyme Ferry continues to operate today.) In 1798–1799, Abisha Woodward of New London, a builder of lighthouses, constructed Warner's mansion with Scamozzi-capped columns flanking a regional variant of a Palladian window with its round tops. The Colonial Revival side porch replicated the house's original details but includes a unique screen design (below). This is one of the finest estates of the lower valley. (Above, ChHS; below, LOC.)

Deacon Jesse Hurd built this granite and brownstone-trimmed Federal-style house around 1812 in Middle Haddam, Connecticut. Hurd was a shipmaster, builder, and investor, merchant in trade with New Yorkers, and a rum distiller. Most notably, he founded the New York Screw Dock Company in 1827. Hurd's company developed patented screw mechanisms for lifting cargo from ship holds, as well as getting vessels onto drydocks for repairs. (MHL.)

In 1849, Henry and Jane Williams Wooster built what was considered the most fashionable new home in Essex, Connecticut, likely designed by architect Henry Austin of New Haven with exotic details. Henry Wooster, with Jeremiah Gladwin, was the owner of the Connecticut River Steam Saw Mill, providing planed wood lumber, moldings, sash, blinds, and doors to builders, as well as wood planks to shipbuilders. Ships were also constructed in their yard near the river. (EsHS.)

The village port of Middle Haddam in East Hampton, Connecticut, was a major Connecticut River shipbuilding center in the 18th and 19th centuries. Here, Samuel Butler, who manufactured marine hardware, built his Greek Revival–style house directly on the river in 1838 (above). After 1855, it was the home of Capt. Edward Simpson. Simpson sailed the river for 35 years, first as captain of the steamer *Champion*, then as pilot and, beginning in 1859, captain of the *City of Hartford*, the luxuriously outfitted steamboat considered the queen of the river. It made three runs weekly between Hartford and New York City for a $1.50 fare. A newspaper claimed Simpson was "universally acknowledged to be one of the most efficient and reliable commanders." By about 1910, Simpson's house overlooked the then-peaceful riverfront landing (below). The glory days of the steamers were quickly passing. (Both, MHL.)

Two

RIVER PRODUCERS

The fertile alluvial soils of the Connecticut River's intervales, often built up between the oxbow twists and turns of its courses, attracted settlers to the valley, led by farmers seeking arable croplands and grassy plains for livestock. Original land grants, based on English precedents, often extended in ribbonlike sections from the floodplain to upper terraces. These home lots typically fronted on community land or shared commons. Only much later would these open spaces be transformed into town greens, around which Americans constructed their meeting houses and mansions. These greens were connected along the valley by roads paralleling the river's course. By the mid-19th century, these parklike settings, surrounded by white clapboarded and stately redbrick homes, came to exemplify New England's charm.

The earliest farming communities were in northern Connecticut and southern Massachusetts. By the end of the 17th century, these spread south to Middletown, Connecticut, and north to Northfield, Massachusetts. The early settlements were challenged by the natives' resistance and retribution for the actual and perceived transgressions by the colonials, leading to deadly raids and conflict. Only after 1750 were more permanent settlements established in the upper valley of Vermont and New Hampshire.

Besides growing agricultural products such as fruit, grains, and vegetables, valley farmers came to specialize in tobacco, flower and vegetable seeds, cider and maple syrup, merino sheep, beef, poultry, eggs, milk, and cheese. By 1900, valley producers enjoyed monopolies on cigars, onions, peaches, and witch hazel. Via the river (and later turnpikes and railroads), they shipped their products to regional markets.

Valley farmsteads often expanded with time and consolidation by marriage. Some evolved into gentleman farms when, especially starting in the late 19th century, industrialists and professionals returned to the valley to establish seasonal retreats from congested cities. These men and women, often returning to ancestral land, created model farms, investing heavily in barns, coops, manure houses, drainage, and fertilizers according to the latest agricultural science. Produce was sent to city homes or sold locally. Often, livestock was specially bred to compete in regional or national competitions as a point of pride.

A national historic landmark in Wethersfield, Connecticut, the Buttolph-Williams House, with its steep roof, hewn second-story overhang, and small casement windows, demonstrates English medieval building techniques typifying early 18th century Connecticut River Valley farmsteads. Built originally around 1711 for tavernkeeper Benjamin Belden, it was restored in 1947. The house served as the inspiration and setting for Elizabeth George Speare's book *The Witch of Blackbird Pond*. (AM.)

Selectman, deacon, and ensign John Sheldon built his farmhouse around 1699 inside the stockade enclosure at Deerfield Plantation (Massachusetts). It was famously the site of an attack by Native Americans and the French in 1704 when Sheldon's wife, Mary, was murdered. It was demolished in 1848 despite preservation efforts, but the front door of the Old Indian House, gouged by hatchets in the attack, was saved. (JLib.)

The earliest portion of this house in South Glastonbury, Connecticut, seen in this c. 1880 photograph, dates to about 1649, built by Lt. John Hollister Jr. It may have originally stood on the bank of the Connecticut River and been moved to its present location about 1721. Hollister lived on the opposite side of the river in Wethersfield, leasing this farm to the Gilbert family. The overhang's carved corbels are rare examples of English architectural precedents. (HGS.)

The Howes brothers of Ashfield, Massachusetts, photographed many river valley residents before their homes between 1886 and 1902, including this young lady in front of the Capt. Jonathan Sheldon farmhouse (built 1723) in Suffield, Connecticut. Jonathan and Mary Sheldon also constructed houses on their 1,100-acre farm for five of their sons, dying "The Happy Pair," as inscribed on their gravestone. Thirty-six acres of the 300-year-old farm are still devoted to agriculture. (KML.)

Venture Smith (née Broteer Furro) was an enslaved West African who purchased his family's freedom. Successfully farming and trading in lumber and fish, he assembled over 100 acres on the Salmon River near the Connecticut River in Haddam Neck, Connecticut. In his book *A Narrative of the Life and Adventures of Venture, A Native of Africa* (1798), Smith told the dramatic story of his journey to freedom and self-sufficiency. This painting of his homestead is based on archaeological investigations of the site. (© 2009, Maggie Arnold.)

Historic preservationists Herb and Sherry Clark saved and restored the architecturally significant First Period Joshua Bushnell House (built in 1678, with a second story added in 1709) in Old Saybrook, Connecticut. Occupied by the Bushnell family for almost 200 years, the 21-acre farm fairly matches the original plot, and with early outbuildings is a rare surviving example of a preindustrial, self-sufficient farmstead. Open to the community, it showcases colonial agricultural methods and life. (OSHS.)

Francis Goodhue built this stately brick Federal-style house about 1804 (above) as the centerpiece of his 2,000-acre estate, including farms and mills, that occupied most of Weathersfield, Vermont's, river oxbow. In 1812, William Jarvis (above inset), retiring US consul to Portugal under Pres. Thomas Jefferson, bought Bow Farm and populated it with imported Holstein cattle, Portuguese swine, and English-bred horses. He also imported thousands of Spanish merino sheep (below) and is credited for their introduction to the country. This led to "merino-mania" speculation and the establishment of Vermont's woolen industry, which dominated its 19th-century agriculture. William's daughter Katherine, with her husband, Leavitt Hunt, inherited the estate, renamed Elmsholme. Hunt, an attorney and photographer, had brothers, architect Richard Morris Hunt and painter William Morris Hunt, who spent time in Weathersfield. (Above, AM; below, VHS.)

From 1752, when built by Moses Porter, until 1955, when a Porter descendant created a foundation to operate it as a museum site, the Porter-Phelps-Huntington House in Hadley, Massachusetts (above), has descended in the same family line for six generations. Atypically, mostly strong daughters took charge of farming operations, aided by enslaved people and indentured servants. Forty Acres, as it was known, is believed to be the first house built on the commons acreage outside the stockades of Hadley. With painted rusticated siding to mimic sandstone and a center hall, the original house was the central valley's showpiece. During the last quarter of the 18th century, Elizabeth Porter Phelps and her husband, Charles Phelps, thoroughly remodeled according to the prevailing architectural tastes, adding the gambrel roof and the ells and connecting the house to new chaise and wood sheds (below). (Both, JLib.)

In the 1890s, Forty Acres and the central river valley was documented by author, illustrator, and photographer Clifton Johnson. His photographs are on the previous page and include the woodshed (above). Forty Acres, later known as Elm Valley, expanded to 600 acres fronting the Connecticut River, but subsequent Phelps and Huntington generations sold off land and visited only in the summer. Below, Episcopal bishop Frederic Dan Huntington, who grew up on the farm, enjoys a tea party with his wife and daughters before the front porch around 1880. In 1949, Dr. James Lincoln Huntington restored the house and removed outbuildings, guided by a historical reinterpretation typical of the Colonial Revival during the first half of the 20th century. The house and original furnishings represent one family's remarkable 300-year association with Forty Acres. (Above, JLib; below, SCUA/UMAL.)

While tobacco was grown throughout the fertile Connecticut River Valley in the 19th and 20th centuries, the six Loomis brothers of Suffield, Connecticut, perfected the art of rolling, packaging, and merchandising their tobacco products, especially cigars, which they shipped throughout the country. Their sons, carrying on the profitable business, constructed grand Italianate villas along Suffield's Main Street. George Loomis built his in 1860 (seen above around 1875). The upper porch's Moorish column tops, the arched window lambrequin valances, and colored glass in the cupola windows lent the house an exotic flavor. Another Loomis in the tobacco-growing business, Charles, constructed his home, also on Main Street in Suffield, in 1862 (below). It is eclectic in its combination of Italianate cross gables, Second Empire tower roofs, and Stick-style expressed framing braces—an early precursor of Victorian architectural excess to follow. (Both, KML.)

In 1872, Henry P. Kent, another wealthy Suffield, Connecticut, merchant involved in the tobacco trade, built a more architecturally consistent house, employing the then-popular Second Empire–style, here interpreted by local architect John C. Mead. It was later the home of important Suffield philanthropist Samuel Reid Spencer. (KML.)

Widow Frances Edwards Hale built this Second Empire–style mansion in 1875–1876 in Glastonbury, Connecticut, a year after her husband, Atwater Hale, a wealthy tobacco farmer, died. Albert Barrows constructed the elaborate home, planned in large part by Frances's son-in-law John Quincy Goodrich, whose family moved in to run the farm. "Nellie" Griswold Goodrich, granddaughter-in-law of Frances, stands in the sideyard in about 1905. (HSG.)

The Simeon Belden House of 1767, with its original Connecticut Valley doorway topped with a broken scroll pediment, was the birthplace of the seed industry of Wethersfield, Connecticut. Here, Simeon's sons Joseph and James, beginning in 1811, developed the Wethersfield Seed Gardens. This business was absorbed by Comstock, Ferre & Company in 1838, and with the later Hart Seed Company, Wethersfield became a center for seed production in the 19th century. (LOC.)

Old Wethersfield, Connecticut, residents, proud of their village of understated colonial homes, may have agreed with the *Connecticut Courant*'s assessment of Silas Robbins's home being constructed in 1872 as a "pretentious . . . ornament to any city." Robbins, a merchant of wholesale and commission box seeds, built his Second Empire–style home fronting the Broad Street Green. It was later the home of contractor Albert Hubbard, who suburbanized Wethersfield with Colonial Revival "Hubbard Homes" in the early 20th century. (AM.)

In 1911, "Peach King" John Howard Hale, reflecting his great success as an orchardist, built his expansive Colonial Revival–style home (above) on a hill in Glastonbury, Connecticut, with distant views to the Connecticut River. Under his direction, the Hale family had vastly expanded its stony 35-acre colonial-period river farm to 500 productive acres. Using natural fertilizing techniques, Hale developed a peach to thrive in New England's harsh climate. Acquiring additional orchards in Georgia, the eccentric and colorful Hale pioneered the sorting, grading, packing, shipping, and marketing of produce, becoming the country's largest peach grower. Hale (below in white hat), with brother and partner George (center) oversaw all operations of the profitable business. The landmark house was later an inn known as Hale House, which specialized in peach ice cream and cake. (Both, HGS.)

The core of this house in Woodstock, Vermont, dates to 1805. It underwent a number of expansions and renovations. It was the childhood home of George Perkins Marsh, author of *Man and Nature* (1864), considered America's first environmentalist work. In 1886, Frederick Billings transformed it in the Queen Anne–style (above) as designed by the nationally recognized architect Henry Hudson Holly, who introduced the style to this country. Frederick Billings, an attorney who made his fortune in San Francisco real estate during the gold rush, later directed the Northern Pacific Railroad's transcontinental expansion. Below, one year after the house was completed, the Billings family and friends pose on the grounds designed by Robert Morris Copeland, noted Boston landscape architect. Inset are, from left to right, (first row) daughter Elizabeth and Frederick's wife, Julia; (second row) daughters Laura and Mary. (All, BFA/WF.)

Frederick Billings expanded the Marsh Estate in Woodstock, Vermont, to 1,100 acres, which were scientifically managed using the latest sustainable methods. Billings, strongly influenced by George Perkins Marsh's writings, reforested woodlots including nearby Mount Tom. He was the first to import purebred Jersey cows from the Isle of Jersey into Vermont, breeding them to win national prizes. He brought Southdown sheep to the farm in 1883 (above). After he died in 1890, Julia and daughters Laura, Mary, and Elizabeth ran the farm with the help of 100 farmhands and manager George Aitken. Some of these workers pose at the barn in 1894 below. Three generations of Billings women ran the farm. Mary's daughter was Mary French Rockefeller, who, with her husband, Laurance Rockefeller, gifted the property for Vermont's first national park, Marsh-Billings-Rockefeller National Historical Park. (Both, BFA/WF.)

Haddam, Connecticut, native Edward Hazen, advertising director of Curtis Publishing Company, became a gentleman dairyman after retiring in 1915. Hazen returned to his parent's homestead, purchasing 500 acres of adjacent Connecticut riverfront farms. This c. 1900 dairy barn, a Haddam landmark with its two cupolas and silos, was the crown jewel of Hazenhurst Farm. The meadows along the river where Hazen's cows once grazed became Haddam Meadows State Park in 1944. One hundred acres were donated to the state by the philanthropic foundation Hazen established in 1925. (HaHS.)

In 1908, Elmer Darling, owner of the Fifth Avenue Hotel in New York City, completed construction of his Burklyn Hall atop Darling Ridge, which straddled the borders of East Burke and Lyndon, Vermont. The massive and opulent Georgian Revival mansion designed by Jardine, Kent & Jardine was the showpiece of his 7,000-acre Mountain View Farm, where Darling produced milk, cheese, and butter that was shipped by railroad to his hotel. (VHS.)

In 1922, Edward Everett Dickinson reconstructed his home (above) in Essex, Connecticut, in an imposing Neoclassical Revival style (below). It included an impressive colonnade across the front and rear porches overlooking Essex's harbor, and was likely designed by New London architect Dudley St. Claire Donnelly. The earlier home was built in 1842 by merchant Charles Smith, and after 1860, enlarged by New Yorker Smith Bellows for his summer home. Bellows, from upriver Middletown, was a contractor specializing in the maintenance of New York City's oil and gas street lights. Until 1979, Dickinson and three generations of his descendants controlled the harvesting and distillation of the indigenous witch hazel shrub in the lower valley, monopolizing the US production of naturally astringent herbal products used in pharmaceuticals and cosmetics. They employed brilliant branding and advertising. The mansion was aptly called Hazelhurst. (Both, EsHS.)

Myron and Rosa Tenney pose proudly with their family before their eccentric Gothic Revival–style farmhouse in Ascutney, Vermont (above around 1906). Their son Romaine, second from right, inherited the 75-acre dairy farm, which he never left except to serve in World War II. Like many Connecticut River Valley homesteads, Tenney's was destroyed with the construction of Interstate Highway 91 between 1960 and 1978, which connected river towns from Middletown, Connecticut, to the Canadian border. Bachelor Romaine Tenney (below) shunned the modernization of his farm, refused to sell his property, and stubbornly resisted the eminent domain order that would have taken his land in 1964. Days after this photograph, he committed suicide in the rear ell of the house. His story in *Yankee* magazine drew national attention to his plight, and to this day, reminds New Englanders of the price they pay for progress. (Both, WVtHS.)

Three

RIVER PATRIOTS AND POLS

Connecticut River Valley men and women contributed to the formation of constitutional systems of governance, served in American wars, and struggled in political and judicial settings to improve and enforce the nation's laws.

The lower valley had its share of Tory sympathizers during the Revolutionary War period, but many others sacrificed their livelihood, and some their lives, for the cause of independence. Col. Charles Johnston, who built his home in Haverhill, New Hampshire, with views across the Valley to the river, was a hero of the Battle of Bennington in 1777. Samuel B. Webb from Wethersfield, Connecticut, served in the war at the sieges of Boston and New York, was George Washington's aide-de-camp (crossing the Delaware in his boat), and was wounded at the Battle of Trenton. Maj. General Samuel Parsons, with a house on Main Street in Middletown, Connecticut, was an early advocate for American independence and perhaps the first to suggest that a Continental Congress be established. Parsons actively engaged in battles in New York and Boston and on Long Island Sound. River valley merchants provisioned the Continental Army with food, munitions, and clothing.

Connecticut River Valley men and women also contributed to the north's victory in the Civil War. General "Fighting Joe" Hooker from Hadley, Massachusetts, commanded the Army of the Potomac. George Ashmun of Springfield, Massachusetts, was Abraham and Mary Lincoln's advisor and confidante, and Lincoln's only civilian pallbearer. In the Spanish-American War, Bradford, Vermont, native Adm. Charles Clark captained the ship *Oregon* to victory at Santiago Bay in 1896, while Rear Adm. William Folger, captain of the USS *New Orleans*, retired to live in Cornish, New Hampshire. Newbury, Vermont, was the childhood home, and Hanover, New Hampshire, the retirement place of "the Other Patton," Ernie Harmon, World War I veteran and fearless tank commander of World War II.

While battles were fought in the name of democracy and freedom, the cherished democratic modes of governance, typical of New England towns, forged valley leaders who went on to serve in statehouses, the courts, and on to Washington, DC. Representatives, senators, judges, cabinet officials, and a president with roots in the river valley left their marks on US history in many varied and important ways.

Col. Samuel Selden, a highly respected farmer, fisherman, and West Indies trader, left the house he built in 1750 at the confluence of Selden Creek and the Connecticut River (above in 1870) to fight to defend New York City from advancing British soldiers in 1776. At the Battle of Kip's Bay, he was wounded and died in captivity. He left behind a widow, Elizabeth Ely Selden, and nine children (two sons had also served in the Revolutionary War). The homestead overlooked the family's extensive Twelve Mile Island Farm in the Selden's Neck section of present-day Hadlyme, Connecticut, and was occupied by five generations of Seldens. The center-chimney Colonial house with high-style Georgian enhancements, including corner quoins and eared window surrounds, was measured and photographed (below) in the 1930s by the Historic American Building Survey. (Above, AM; below, LOC.)

In 1777, Benjamin Ruggles Woodbridge (above inset) led a contingent of men to fight at Boston's Battle of Bunker Hill. He later served at the second Battle of Saratoga, considered a critical turning point in the Revolutionary War. Woodbridge, South Hadley, Massachusetts's, wealthiest bachelor (owning a rum still, sawmill, and gristmill), built this grand Georgian-style house in 1788. The three-story, gambrel-roofed mansion came to be known as The Sycamores. It was later a boys' school and then, for 65 years, the center of a farm operated by the Montague family. It was restored with Colonial Revival touches by Rose Hollingsworth for a summer home and later served as a dormitory for the women of Mount Holyoke College (below, with boyfriends, preparing for a hayride around 1950). (Both, MHCA&SC.)

Alexander King, who built this house in 1764 on Main Street in Suffield, Connecticut, was typical of many lower river valley, Yale-educated men who dedicated their lives to public service. Dr. King was a selectman, town clerk, justice of the peace, general assembly deputy, and a delegate to the 1788 state convention ratifying the US Constitution. The West and Wallace families pose before the house around 1910. (KML.)

The c. 1725 John McCurdy House in Old Lyme, Connecticut, saw many changes, including Gothic Revival touches around 1860. Reputed to have been visited by George Washington and General LaFayette, its most important association is with influential public servant Judge Charles J. McCurdy (inset, 1797–1891), who served as a state representative and senator, lieutenant governor, superior court judge, and US minister to the Austrian Empire. (AM.)

Connecticut lawyer Oliver Ellsworth assisted with the drafting of the US Constitution. A US senator, he wrote the Judiciary Act establishing the federal court system. Washington appointed Ellsworth the third chief justice of the Supreme Court. Under Pres. John Adams, he negotiated a treaty with France preventing war. Samuel Denslow built Ellsworth's house in 1781 in Windsor, Connecticut, with an addition to the right by Thomas Hayden in 1790 and a colonnade added in 1836. Ellsworth called his home Elmwood, and planted 13 elm trees, one for each state, some of which were alive as of 1910 (above). Ralph Earl's 1792 painting of Ellsworth and his wife, Abigail Wolcott Ellsworth (below), includes a view of their house through the window. (Above, WiHS; below, gift of the Ellsworth heirs, Wadsworth Atheneum Museum of Art.)

Connecticut River Valley merchants supported the armies of the Revolutionary War in many ways. The original c. 1761 core of this house in Suffield, Connecticut, was constructed by Tory sympathizer Shem Burbank, whose business trading in goods from England suffered during the Revolution. In 1788, he sold the property to Oliver Phelps (left), a patriot who was at the Battle of Lexington and also served as a deputy commissar organizing supplies for General Washington's troops. Phelps then served Massachusetts (Suffield was then a part of that state) at its Constitution Convention and represented his community in both the Massachusetts House and Senate. Phelps reconstructed the Burbank house with a new gambrel roof and matching addition in 1794, probably by master valley architect and builder Thomas Hayden, with classical decorative features attributed to the young Asher Benjamin. (Above, KML; left, OCHS.)

The interior design of Oliver Phelps's addition included imported French wallpaper (as seen in the parlor above), making this house singularly important as an early example of high-style coastal fashions based on English architectural books. The west parlor's plasterwork and wallpaper went to Winterthur Museum and were replicated here. Historian William Hosley describes the addition as "the first fully developed neoclassical environment in the Connecticut Valley." Phelps could also afford to import fine furniture from Boston, as he was the largest landowner in the country, controlling millions of acres in western New York, Ohio, and elsewhere. However, in 1802, he was forced to sell the Suffield mansion as a result of land speculation losses. Asahel Hatheway and his descendants occupied the house until 1956, having constructed the fourth gambrel-roofed wing to the rear (below). The house is currently managed by Connecticut Landmarks. (Both, LOC.)

In 1752, housewright Judah Wright built this early center-hall Georgian house in Wethersfield, Connecticut, for Joseph Webb, a successful West Indies trader (above around 1940). It is believed that the tall gambrel-roofed attic space housed Webb's imported goods and enslaved Africans. After his death in 1761, his widow, Mehitabel Nott Webb (whose own family was in the trade), ran his business. Joseph Webb Jr. was also a merchant, and his wife, Abigail Chester, inherited the house. As a locus of social life in Wethersfield, their home became known as Hospitality Hall. In May 1781, George Washington and the comte de Rochambeau met in the room pictured below in 1939 at the invitation of Webb's brother Samuel B. Webb to devise the military strategy that led to the siege of Yorktown that ended the Revolutionary War. (Above, CTSL; below, WDSM.)

By 1770, lawyer and politician Silas Deane completed construction of his house in Wethersfield, Connecticut, next door to that of his first wife, Mehitabel, who had become the widow of Joseph Webb. Deane supervised Webb's trading operation, which included smuggling to bypass the Navigation Acts imposed by England on the colonies. He was a Connecticut delegate to the First Continental Congress of 1774 and America's first diplomat to France during the Revolutionary War, secretly securing aid for the patriot cause. The house was distinguished by a rare, early piazza across the facade (above) and a dramatic stair hall with differently turned balusters leading to a second-floor balcony (below). Deane, enmeshed in financial hardships, political controversies, and intrigues, died in England in 1789, his reputation in tatters (only to be resuscitated by the US government and future historians). The Colonial Dames received the house from the Fenn family in 1959, and it was restored to the 1776 period, when Deane left for Europe, never to return to the house he built. (Both, WDSM.)

Built around 1750 and later a tavern, tenement, and warehouse, the Old Constitution House in Windsor, Vermont (above) was rescued by local preservationists in 1914 and restored by the state after its acquisition in 1961. Representatives met here in 1777 to adopt the constitution that created the Vermont Republic from land claimed by four adjacent colonies. The Federal-style Francis Gardner House (built around 1808) across the river in Walpole, New Hampshire (below), later was the home of attorney, judge, and politician Stephen Rowe Bradley. As the Vermont Republic's attorney general, Bradley negotiated its acceptance as the Union's 14th state in 1791. He served as the new state's first US senator and senate president pro tempore, and crafted the 12th Amendment to the Constitution that defined the process to elect the US president and vice president. (Above, VHS; below, WaHS.)

Delaware native Commodore Thomas Macdonough Jr. commanded 14 ships, and his naval victory over the British fleet on Lake Champlain at Plattsburgh in 1814 led to the end of the War of 1812. He was a national hero, honored with the congressional medal; his portrait at right was painted by Gilbert Stuart. Macdonough came to Middletown, Connecticut, with Commodore Isaac Hull and oversaw gunboat operations there. In 1812, he married a local woman, Lucy Ann Shaler. Seven years later, he constructed this imposing Federal-style house on Main Street. Its generous piazza with unusually early cast-iron column capitols was topped with a balcony from which one could view the Connecticut River. (Right, NGA; below, MCHS.)

In 1846, wool merchant John Brown came from Ohio to live in Springfield, Massachusetts, where he sought to organize Connecticut River Valley sheep-growers to coordinate for higher wool sale prices abroad. Here, he associated with African American church leaders and antislavery activists; his home (above around 1884) was said to be a station of the Underground Railroad. Black abolitionist Frederick Douglass visited and was in awe of Brown's humble lifestyle. In Springfield, Brown, radicalized, founded the League of Gileadites to resist the capture of fugitive slaves. This abolition activity led to his failed raid on the federal armory at Harper's Ferry. Convicted of treason and executed in 1859, Brown is considered a martyred hero in the river valley. African American photographer Augustus Washington made this daguerreotype of Brown in 1846–1847 at his Hartford studio. (Above, WMSH; left, NPG.)

Newspaperman and politico Gideon Welles (inset) was born in the house seen above, constructed in 1783 in Glastonbury, Connecticut, by his grandfather Samuel Welles. Gideon Welles was appointed by Pres. Abraham Lincoln as his secretary of the Navy from 1861–1869 (calling him "Father Neptune"). Welles was responsible for doubling and modernizing the Navy, overseeing critical naval operations that helped win the Civil War. He and his wife, Mary Jane, were loyal confidantes of Abraham and Mary Todd Lincoln. Gideon was at the president's side when he died. In retirement and living in Hartford, Welles poses below, seated in a chair at right with Mary Jane, third from left, surrounded by family at his Glastonbury birthplace. The house, remaining in the Welles family until 1932, was moved in 1936; its preservation led to the formation of the Historical Society of Glastonbury. (Both, HSG.)

Gen. Joseph King Fenno Mansfield (left in a photograph by Matthew Brady) was an Army engineer overseeing the construction of forts and harbor defenses around the country, also serving as Army inspector general of the western territories. He fought in the Mexican-American War and, during the Civil War, commanded shore batteries at the battle of the ironclad ships *Merrimack* and *Monitor*. He later was in charge of the defenses of Washington, DC. He died a national hero leading the XII Corps at the Battle of Antietam in 1862. Seen below around 1895, his Federal-style house on Main Street in Middletown, Connecticut, was constructed in 1810 by Robert Watkinson, a dry goods merchant. The house was occupied by Joseph and his wife, Louisa's, descendants until 1959. Since then it has been the home of the Middlesex County Historical Society. (Left, NARA; below, MCHS.)

After a fire destroyed his Longmeadow, Massachusetts, home in 1845, Roderick Burnham (below left) built the Gothic Revival–style home above using East Longmeadow brownstone. Set amidst 16 picturesque acres with distant views of the Connecticut River, the house emulated Washington Irving's well-known Hudson River villa Sunnyside, with its unusual stepped-crow dormer gables, as well as Ida Cottage in Troy, New York, designed by A.J. Davis. Roderick's 21-year-old son Howard (below right) was killed at the Civil War Battle of Chickamauga. Roderick, faithful to Howard's parting wishes, retrieved his son's body from its hasty burial in Chattanooga, bringing Howard home to be interred in the nearby cemetery in Longmeadow. Howard Burnham's uncle was Gen. Joseph K.F. Mansfield (see the previous page), and Howard was due to serve as Mansfield's aide-de-camp. (Above, LHS. Below left, LHS; below right, AM.)

Salmon P. Chase's 1808 birthplace and boyhood home, built around 1790, is a landmark in Cornish, New Hampshire. It is depicted in the engraving above that accompanied his biography published after his death in 1874. Chase (left) was an ardent antislavery attorney, and a US senator and governor of Ohio. President Lincoln appointed him treasury secretary, and he organized the national banking system, adding "In God We Trust" to American currency. He was later an important chief justice of the US Supreme Court (but always an ambitious and perennial presidential candidate). He held the distinction of swearing in Pres. Andrew Johnson in 1865 after Lincoln's assassination and presiding over Johnson's impeachment trial three years later. The house associated with Chase and his distinguished legal and political career is a national historic landmark. (Above, AM; left, NPG.)

This imposing brick Federal-style house in Walpole, New Hampshire was built in 1812 by Josiah Bellows II, a talkative tavernkeeper known as "Slick Si." Details were inspired by architect Asher Benjamin's work across the Connecticut River in Windsor, Vermont. It was the childhood home of Unitarian minister Frederick Newman Knapp (above inset). During the Civil War, Knapp served the US Sanitary Commission in Washington, DC, as the superintendent of the Special Relief Service, organized to assist disabled Union veterans. His work went unsung, but his eulogist wrote, "If the good done by Mr. Knapp in this way were known, the news of his death would lead Congress to adjourn and the bells would toll throughout the land." His widow, Lucia Alden Knapp, is pictured below in a room with original French scenic wallpaper "Monuments of Paris." (All, DRHS.)

The Gothic Revival–style home pictured above in Strafford, Vermont, was the home of Justin Morrill, which he designed and built in 1848–1851. Morrill served in the US Congress as a representative and senator for 44 years and is best known as the author of the Land-Grant Acts of 1862 and 1890, facilitating public colleges and universities. Morrill, self-taught in architecture and construction, was also instrumental in the completion of the Washington Monument, the erection of the Library of Congress, and the landscaping of the US Capitol grounds. In the c. 1890 photograph below, he poses on the rear porch; from left to right are Justin, wife Ruth Barrell Swan, dog Trump, son James, and sister-in-law Louise Swan. To the left is a mercury garden globe, very much in fashion at the time. (Above, LOC; below, VDHP/96-B-2.)

Justin Morrill expanded the house in about 1858, enlarging the dining room, adding the castellated front porch (previous page) and the library (at right above, seen in 1959). Hand-carved mahogany trim with Gothic Revival details enhanced the house's interior rooms, which Morrill, while referring to the architectural pattern books of his day, customized in ways that suited his taste. Although he mostly lived in Washington, DC, he spent his downtime here in Strafford. Morrill was photographed in 1889 in his library (below), the focal point of which was a bay window with colorful lithophane panels. The Justin Morrill Homestead, with many original Morrill furnishings, farm outbuildings, and gardens, also designed by Morrill, is a national historic landmark, Vermont's first. (Above, LOC; below, VDHP/Morrill family.)

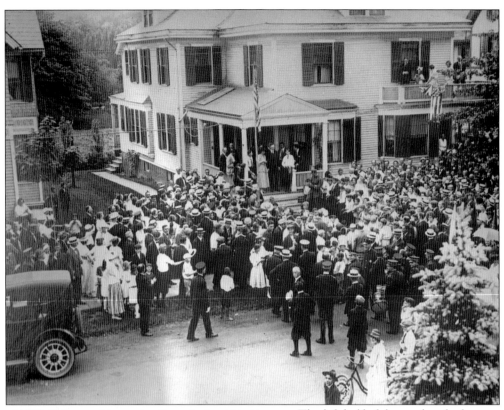

The left half of the modest duplex in Northampton, Massachusetts, pictured above was the home of frugal Yankee Calvin Coolidge from 1906 to 1930, rented for $27 a month. The plain Colonial Revival–style home, built in 1901, was where he lived from the time that the fiscally conservative attorney rose meteorically from Northampton councilman to mayor, state representative, lieutenant governor, governor, vice president, and president of the United States (when not in the White House). Seen above on July 27, 1920, Governor Coolidge (on the porch) is notified that he was nominated to be vice president. Coolidge recalled, "so long as I lived there, I could be independent and serve the public without ever thinking that I could not maintain my position if I left office." To the left is Coolidge with sons Calvin Jr. (left) and John. (Both, FLib/CCPL&M.)

THE BEECHES.
RESIDENCE OF
EX.PRES.COOLIDGE

Seeking privacy from sightseers who came in droves to see the Massasoit Street home of the ex-president, in 1930, the Coolidges purchased The Beeches in Northampton (above). The Arts and Crafts–style home was constructed in 1915 by Henry MacCracken, a Smith College professor, but was occupied mostly by the Comey family. The 16-room house, surrounded by beech trees and nine acres with a view of Northampton Meadows and the Connecticut River, was described by Coolidge as "a modest place with a little land." Below, around Thanksgiving 1930, Grace and Calvin Coolidge greet Santa Claus and local schoolchildren, kicking off the 24th annual sale of Christmas seals to benefit the National Tuberculosis League. The event was covered by many film production companies making promotional shorts to be shown in theaters. Three years later, Coolidge died here of a sudden heart attack at age 60. (Both, HN.)

The Francis Bushnell House (built in 1745) in Chester, Connecticut (above), was the seasonal home of Constance Baker Motley ("CBM") and her family from 1965 to 2009. Motley, an NAACP lawyer who successfully litigated over 200 desegregation cases in southern courts, was the first black woman to argue a case before the Supreme Court, the first African American to serve in the New York State Senate (seen left in 1964), and as borough president of Manhattan. In 1966, President Johnson nominated her to serve as a federal judge—yet another first for an African American woman. Motley was chief judge of the Federal District Court, Southern District of New York, where CBM's rulings advanced rights for women, workers, and prisoners. In 2018, the home and adjacent Motley family land (previously designated the Judge Motley Preserve), was placed on the Connecticut Freedom Trail. (Above, ChHS; left, LOC.)

Four

RIVER MAKERS

Trading between the lower and upper Connecticut River Valley towns was always limited by the river's shallow and shifting waters, unpredictable spring flooding, challenging rapids, and winter ice jams. Moreover, international trade competition, the 1807 Embargo Act, and the War of 1812 with England devastated lower valley shipping and its profits. Newly dug canals, faster steamships, and turnpike and railroad construction ensured the end of the era of the sailing ships—the schooners and the brigs—that were essential to the fortunes of the river gods.

However, the natural resources presented by the Connecticut River Valley's topography were harnessed for manufacturing, reflecting Yankee ingenuity and hard work. Countless tributary streams, descending from the valley's foothills, were diverted and dammed in order to turn milling wheels that powered local industry in the valley. Where diversion of streams to irrigate farms and summer droughts impinged these streams' flow, steam engines fueled by the region's bounteous woodlands and imported coal were employed to boost manufacturing efficiencies. Towns and cities without water power could now consider expanding their manufacturing capability as well. Young women, followed by European immigrants, provided the cheap labor, skills, and experience required to operate the mills. As the nation expanded quickly to the west, new markets were created for their products.

Fresh fortunes were made from the manufacture of a wide variety of products. Valley manufactures included buttons, cloth, silk thread, elastic webbing, pewter, silver cutlery, brass fittings, swords, rifles, pistols, tools, ice skates, ivory piano keys, cast iron toys, scales, water pumps, shaving soap, bicycles, motorcycles, automobiles, sail and steamships, and prefabricated house frames. The Connecticut River itself was diverted and harnessed at places like Turners Falls and Holyoke to create vast industrial communities. Gigantic mills, utilitarian millworkers' housing, and owners' and superintendents' mansions came to dominate many late-19th-century valley landscapes. The mineral-rich valley also offered up to its quarrymen such diverse stone products as whetstone for tool sharpening, feldspar, brownstone for buildings, and granite for streets and curbs—all shipped nationwide.

Historic houses reflected this new wealth. The Greek Revival style was employed by the first manufacturing entrepreneurs, but as fashions changed and building technologies improved, 19th- and early-20th-century men and women of industry constructed their homes in new and fashionable architectural styles that reflected their nouveau riche status, community leadership, and cultural aspirations.

After constructing a mill on Deep Hollow Brook in Chester, Connecticut, for the manufacture of gimlets, Charles Daniels built his house and matching stable next door overlooking the brook. Daniels shipped his products to Boston, New York, and Philadelphia via the Connecticut River. The house's construction probably dates to soon after his second marriage, to Abigail Gilbert, in 1832. Its cosmopolitan design was perhaps modeled after English Regency park lodges. (ChHS.)

Arrayed on a raised terrace, three of the original four Greek Revival homes of Claremont, New Hampshire's, industrialists remain as legacies of the early 1830s' "Speculation Times," when the upper valley boomed with new manufacturing ventures. Aaron Howland built these identical homes about 1836 for, from left to right, Charles Putnam, Simeon Ide, Ormond Dutton (demolished), and Henry Russell—men involved in paper, book, and satinet manufacturing in town. (AM.)

Joel Hayden built this Greek Revival–style house about 1828 across the road from his factories on the Mill River in Williamsburg, Massachusetts. Here, with different partners, he manufactured assorted cotton goods, buttons, pens, and brass fittings. His brother and partner Josiah constructed a near duplicate next door 10 years later. The houses, with flanking wings, were sophisticated for their time and represented the mill owners' wealth and community status. (LOC.)

This 1874 photograph of the matching Joel Hayden (right) and Josiah Hayden houses in Haydenville, as the mill village of Williamsburg, Massachusetts, came to be known, was taken soon after the Mill River's reservoir dam failed. The 30-foot-high surging waters destroyed the river's mills and many homes, killing 139 people. A boiler from the Hayden factory floated to Joel Hayden's front yard, overseen here by Pinkerton guards that the Haydens hired to prevent looting. (WMHS.)

The 1874 Mill River flood destroyed William Skinner's Unquomonk Silk Mill in the Skinnerville section of Williamsburg, Massachusetts. His ostentatious Second Empire–style home, designed by Northampton architect William Fenno Pratt in 1868, was essentially spared (above left). After much speculation about whether or not he would rebuild his mill, Skinner relocated his production from the tributary of the Connecticut River to Holyoke, Massachusetts. He also took his 12,000-square-foot house, disassembled and moved in pieces on 25 railroad cars and remodeled by architect Pratt. At left, Skinner and his wife, Sarah, enjoy the front porch enclosed with trellis work that they installed in the 1880s to facilitate the wisteria vines that eventually covered most of the house (above right). (Both, WMA.)

William Skinner and Sons' satin mills were powered by the Holyoke Water Company's massive project to divert the waterpower of the Connecticut River with dams and canals. Skinner's factory became the world's largest satin manufacturer and made his seven children wealthy valley philanthropists. Wistariahurst, as they christened their homestead in 1904, was remodeled and enlarged in 1913 by Ruth Isabelle "Belle" Skinner. Clarence Luce, a New York architect of many Newport, Rhode Island, mansions, assisted her. The Music Room seen above in 1933 displayed Belle's collection of rare musical instruments, now at Yale University. In 1927, another addition included the Great Hall (below), graced with portraits of William and Sarah Skinner. Katharine Skinner Kilborne and her heirs donated the estate to the City of Holyoke in 1959. The 26-room mansion, now the Wistariahurst Museum, is a historic house and popular event venue. (Both, WMA.)

Overlooking the Connecticut River in Orford, New Hampshire, are seven extraordinary Federal period homes in a row. The earliest was the Obadiah Noble House (built in 1773), to which Samuel Morey made major additions after 1804 (above). Morey was a pioneer of steam-powered paddlewheel boats on the river in the 1790s, receiving patents for related inventions. Later, he developed the earliest documented internal combustion engine in the country. Orford's substantial Ridge Houses, built between 1805 and 1840 on the raised terrace originally owned by Morey, were associated with the Howard, Hinkley, Willard, Wilcox, Rogers, and Wheeler families. The homes were influenced in their designs and details by the work and publications of the valley's master carpenter and architect Asher Benjamin. The southernmost home (below) of merchant John Wheeler, built in 1816, may have been designed by Benjamin himself. (Above, AM; below, LOC.)

Bradford, Vermont, entrepreneur Asa Low, who owned a brick kiln, grist and paper mills, and a general store, expanded merchant Micah Barron's house with a portico in the Greek Revival style after 1824. It sat on a slope overlooking the valley to the east. The pediment included a recessed balcony within an elliptical arched opening. The gable loggia became an interesting architectural element duplicated throughout the upper valley. (VHS.)

The Trotter House was a hostelry in Bradford, Vermont, built in 1846 around Capt. William Trotter's home by Asa Low, who anticipated the railroad coming to Bradford. Its pedimented front with a recessed balcony was similar to that of Asa Low's House (previous photograph). The Trotter House, like many inns along the valley, advertised "surrounding scenery . . . second to none in the Connecticut Valley," but burned down in 1887. (BradHS.)

The first brick house in Essex, Connecticut (pictured around 1910), was built around 1806 by shipbuilder Richard Hayden. Essex (then Potopaug) was a major shipbuilding center on the Connecticut River. The Hayden homes occupied much of this side of Main Street. Hayden Shipyard and Richard Hayden's fortunes, however, were devastated by the British attack in the War of 1812, but Hayden's house and his chandlery across the street, built in 1813, remain. (EsHS.)

Richard Hayden added the third floor to a relocated house of 1776 vintage but sold it to Ethan Bushnell in 1806 when his new brick house was completed (see previous photograph). Bushnell opened an inn here and numerous additions were made, including attaching a c. 1738 schoolhouse to create a taproom. Hayden's house is now the Griswold Inn, an Essex, Connecticut, landmark and one of the oldest continuously operating inns in the country. (EsHS.)

Erastus Brainerd Sr. bought this house overlooking the Connecticut River at Portland, Connecticut, in 1851, a year after establishing the most successful brownstone quarry there. In the 19th century, most of the country's brownstone was quarried in Portland. The Greek Revival–style house with side wings was built in 1830 and was the childhood home of Elizabeth Hart Jarvis, who married arms-maker Samuel Colt. It was later the home of the Gildersleeve family, Portland shipbuilders. (MCHS.)

In 1876, spendthrift Ely Ely-Goddard constructed his eccentric Swiss-style house in the midst of his very productive Ely Copper Mine in Vershire, Vermont. The balconies and belvedere may have been designed for keeping eyes on the mine's operations. Ely-Goddard hosted lavish parties here for his wealthy friends from New York and Newport. After the mine's failure, the house, sold for $150, was moved to the shore of Lake Fairlee, Vermont. (VHS.)

Chauncey Shepherd constructed the house seen above on a bluff overlooking the river in Springfield, Massachusetts, for David Ames Jr. in 1826. Forty years later, he remodeled it for Ames's son-in-law, attorney Solomon Gordon, keeping the original portico that copied the Byers House (see page 146). The portico was destroyed by a tornado in 2011. Ames Jr. continued the business of his father David Ames Sr., who had pioneered the paper industry in the river valley. In 1828, Ames Sr. had Shepherd construct the nearby house (below) for his other son John Ames as a wedding inducement. John, who advanced the family business with mechanical paper-making inventions, never married or lived here. In 1885, the Dickinson family remodeled, with the addition of the side colonnade and porte cochère (pictured in 1893). (Both, WMSH.)

In 1832, Orrin Thompson (above inset), founder of Enfield, Connecticut's, extensive 19th-century carpet industry, constructed this impressively austere home with its flanking wings. An Indo-Saracenic cupola was added for panoramic sightseeing over the river valley to the west. Thompson's daughter Julia, an avid photographer, probably snapped the view below of her mother, Love (in black), sister Laura (driving), and sister Elizabeth (holding parasol) out for a ride behind the house. Laura and her husband, Harry Grant Allen, Connecticut's surgeon general during the Civil War, inherited the estate. Their son Thompson later established here a gentleman's farm specializing in Jersey cattle. The house was subsequently owned by Springfield, Massachusetts, native Wilbur F. Young, who remodeled it in 1916 with Colonial Revival flourishes to serve as his country home, Long View. (Both, courtesy of Hannah Criser, from the archives of Margaret Prall Grant.)

The Carter brothers pose before their home, Lionhurst, in Lebanon, New Hampshire, above. They continued father Henry W. Carter's dry goods business and, after 1870, developed a national market for their famous Carter's Overalls. Their new factory and store was constructed in 1884 (above right). Henry W. Carter (above inset), the "Prince of Yankee Peddlers," had been a traveling merchant, distributing his wares by fancy wagons around New England. His Italianate-style house was built about 1848 by Henry Campbell, a railroad engineer. Campbell superintended the Northern Railroad's Connecticut River bridge and, in 1836, patented the 4-4-0 locomotive that became the standard for American train design during most of the 19th century. After a fire in 1895, the house was rebuilt with a new corner tower and remodeled in the Colonial Revival style (below). (Both, LHS.)

The Italianate-style house of 1860 pictured above in 1890 in East Haddam, Connecticut, with its massive square tower topped with a mansard roof, was Luther Boardman's home. Boardman founded Connecticut's silversmithing industry in East Haddam, where he manufactured his patented Britannia silverware spoons. From nearby Goodspeed Landing, Boardman shipped his nickel- and silver-plated flat cutlery down the Connecticut River to ports throughout the country and abroad, becoming one of the town's major employers during the second half of the 19th century. He was also a major investor in the Connecticut Valley Railroad and the Hartford and Long Island Steamboat Company. The house with the more fanciful octagonal tower next door (seen below) was the c. 1875 home of his son Norman, who partnered with his father in the plating business, in mills along the streams that fed the Connecticut River. (Both, EHHS.)

It may be said that Samuel Williston's c. 1848 Regency-style home in Easthampton, Massachusetts, was the house that buttons built. The ingenuity of Williston's cloth-covered buttons, manufactured with special machinery, is attributed to his wife, Emily (inset). With their wealth, the Willistons went on to found Williston Academy and fund Mount Holyoke and Grinnell Colleges, among other philanthropic endeavors. (AM.)

Since 1832, the four Bevin brothers were the most successful small bell makers of the many bell manufacturers of East Hampton, Connecticut, where most of the nation's small cast bells were made. The Bevins produced globe sleighbells, handbells, and cowbells, and today their company is the oldest small bell maker in the country. In 1872, Philo Bevin (inset) constructed this fashionable Second Empire–style mansion atop Barton Hill in East Hampton. (AM.)

In 1853, John Stoddard employed architect Richard Upjohn to design this Italianate-style house in Brattleboro, Vermont. Stoddard summered here, his wealth derived from his South Carolina cotton plantations where he employed enslaved blacks and funded Confederate causes. The house, however, is associated with Julius Estey, who called it Florence Terrace (after his wife, Florence). Julius's father, Jacob, founded the Estey Organ Company in Brattleboro, a manufacturer of reed and pipe organs for over 100 years. (BHS.)

In 1868, James Ray, a wealthy owner of a coffin trimmings manufactory, commissioned Jabez Comstock to design his Italianate-style house atop his Ray Hill Farm overlooking Goodspeed Landing in East Haddam, Connecticut. Comstock, from nearby Hadlyme, was the architect of two other Connecticut River landmarks: the Goodspeed Opera House built in 1877, and the 1870 Fenwick Hall Hotel in Old Saybrook, Connecticut. James Ray died in 1887, apparently poisoned by red aniline dye in his stockings. (EHHS.)

Starting in 1849, James Baker Williams manufactured Genuine Yankee Soap, the first shaving soap sold in a mug, in Glastonbury, Connecticut. The success of his innovation was reflected in 1859 when he built his Italianate-style brick mansion (above) near his mill, designed by engineer Lucius Thayer. It was a local joke that Williams (above inset) never used his own product. His son David formulated Ivorine soap, creating a separate business that eventually merged with his father's. This product was later marketed as Ivory soap by Proctor & Gamble. David's house (below), erected in 1892 near his father's—with its towers and undulating roof and wall surface treatments—is one of the finest examples of the Queen Anne style transitioning to the Shingle style in the Connecticut River Valley. A subsequent owner named the estate Heulrhod (or Sunny Bank). (Both, HGS.)

The interiors of David Williams's house (library and stair hall above) were typical of the period, finished with dark wood paneling, ornate turnings, and many built-ins. In 1905, David's brother and partner, Samuel, not to be outdone, constructed nearby on a secluded 25 acres a grander Southern Colonial–style mansion (below) complete with a personal golf course. Hartford architects Davis & Brooks, designers of municipal buildings such as libraries and city halls, get credit for Williams's 25-room mansion. The Williams family company went on to market other well-known men's toiletries such as Aqua Velva and Lectric Shave and was Glastonbury's largest employer for many years. Samuel Williams's house was later the home of Dr. Samuel Rentsch, who invented, among other things, the Benthic Explorer submarine, which he tested in 1978 in the Connecticut River. (Both, HGS.)

James and Lena Hartness constructed this fine example of the Shingle style at Springfield, Vermont, in 1904. The house's bold massing, varied window types and configurations, shingled surfaces, and fieldstone base are hallmarks of the style. Hartness directed the Jones and Lampson Machine Tool Company, patenting 119 devices, including the flat turret lathe, safety razor, and telescopes. From Springfield to Hartford, Connecticut, the river valley was known as "Precision Valley" due to the success of master tool and die makers like Hartness. An avid amateur astronomer, he constructed an equatorial tracking telescope observatory in the yard, connected to the house by an underground labyrinth of tunnels and rooms. Hartness was also one of the country's first aircraft pilots. He constructed Springfield's airfield, and in 1927, hosted Charles Lindberg at his home after the young hero's transatlantic flight (left). (Both, SAHS.)

Constructed in 1845–1847 under the supervision of the Springfield (Massachusetts) Armory's commanding officer Maj. James Wolfe Ripley, this costly Regency-style house dominated Armory Hill and the city below. After completion of the Commandant's House, Ripley (inset) was tried by a military court for extravagant spending on the "magnificent palace" (among other allegations of government waste), but was exonerated. The Springfield Armory produced most of the US military's small arms until closing in 1968. (SANHSA.)

Augustus Hazard constructed this grand Italianate-style Enfield, Connecticut, mansion in 1848, pictured in 1875. Hazard (inset) established the Hazard Powder Company, which supplied half the Union's gunpowder during the Civil War. His milltown of 200 buildings on 400 acres, called Hazardville, was aptly named due to the dangers inherent in manufacturing gunpowder. Samuel Colt, Jefferson Davis (then US secretary of war), and Daniel Webster visited the Hazard home. (EnHS.)

Samuel and Elizabeth Hart Jarvis Colt constructed their mansion, Armsmear, overlooking their new gun armory, the Colt Patent Fire Arms Company, which was adjacent to the Connecticut River in Hartford, Connecticut (above). The manufactory was then the largest of its kind in the world. Here, the famous machine-made Colt .45 caliber revolving barrel gun that "won the west" originated. Undoubtedly the most palatial estate of its period in the entire river valley, the Italianate-style Colt House (seen below in 1907), designed in part by Octavius Jordan, was completed in 1857 and expanded with Moorish-style additions in 1861. A local newspaper described the plans as "quite Napoleonic." It overlooked 106 acres of landscaped grounds, enhanced with formal gardens, extensive greenhouses, artificial ponds, reproductions of famous sculptures, a deer park, and live peacocks. (Above, AM. Below, LOC; inset, AM.)

From 1891 to 1898, Daniel Wesson, co-founder of the Smith & Wesson firearms company, built the grandest urban house in the Connecticut River Valley. The palatial Springfield, Massachusetts, mansion was designed by Bruce Price (Edwin Parlett, contractor, and Adam Ganson, mason) in the Chateauesque mode. It combined the French Renaissance chateau style with Scottish Baronial details in pink granite with red-slate roofs. The sumptuously finished rooms (entrance stair hall below) each featured a distinct fireplace mantelpiece in marble. The castle was enhanced with the most modern conveniences, including a hydraulic elevator. In 1905, Black Hand gang members threatened to dynamite the house unless Wesson paid a ransom. The plot, however, was thwarted by armed policemen who encircled the house. After 1915, the mansion was the home of the exclusive Colony Club but was lost to fire in 1966. (Both, WMSH.)

In 1913, Springfield, Massachusetts, bicycle manufacturer George Hendee, anticipating his retirement, began assembling 460 acres of farmland on the west side of the Connecticut River in the Mapleton village of Suffield, Connecticut, near its border with Massachusetts. By 1916, he completed, high above the river, a 100-foot-long Mediterranean-style villa designed by Springfield architect Max Westhoff and built by Napoleon Russell (above). Greenhouses supplied plantings for the extensively landscaped grounds designed by landscape architect Carl Rust Parker. Below, George Hendee enjoys his garden pavilion in about 1927. With panoramic views over the valley and a mile of riverfront, in 1914, a journalist called George Hendee's estate "a site for the gods." Hendee's Hilltop Manor was demolished in 1961 after a portion of the property was sold to a private college for the construction of a dormitory. (Both, FoFAH.)

Young George Hendee was a high-wheel cycle-racing hero (above left). In 1897, he founded the Hendee Manufacturing Company in Springfield, Massachusetts, to build his American Indian Safety chain-driven bicycles outfitted with equally sized wheels. Hendee improved and marketed motorized pacer cycles for racing, and with Carl Oscar Hedström (see next entry), spun off the Indian Motocycle Company to mass-produce motorcycles. Above right, he recalls his early racing days with a high-wheeler at Hilltop Manor. In 1914, Hendee built a 19,000-square-foot Colonial Revival–style dairy barn designed by architect Max Westhoff (below). The stanchion barn featured a high entrance flanked by ceramic-lined silos, and other agricultural amenities that demonstrated the latest scientific principles. Hendee raised leghorn chickens and Guernsey cows, known nationally as "Hilltop Butterfats." (Above, FoFAH; below, RPC.)

About 1902, Carl Oscar Hedström bought the John Isham Worthington House, a c. 1845 Greek Revival house (above) on Main Street in Portland, Connecticut, high on a hill with distant views of the Connecticut River. With Springfield, Massachusetts, architect F.M. Knowlton, Hedström expanded it in the Colonial Revival style. In a shop across the river in Middletown, Hedström, a nationally recognized racing bicyclist and mechanic, built in 1901 what many consider to be the prototype of the first motorcycle in America. Hedström (below, posed in his driveway) partnered with another famous racing cyclist, bicycle manufacturer George Hendee, establishing the Indian Motocycle Company in Springfield. There, in 1902, Hedström's motorcycle design went into production as the first mass-produced motorcycle. Indian became the largest manufacturer of motorcycles worldwide. (Both, SAY&CY.)

Carl Oscar Hedström's motorcycle racing career, with national titles for speed and distance records, led to technical innovations that won his Indian Motocycle Company much publicity. Above, in 1916, according to a motorcycle trade paper, is an "Indian chiefs pow wow" at Hedström's "modern farm" in Portland. The sales managers are, from left to right, J.H. O'Brien, Frank Weschler, J.A. Priest, and E.M. Jackson, with Hedström. While Hedström continued to benefit from his patents, notably for an efficient motorcycle engine, carburetor, and throttle grip, in 1913, he retired from the company to concentrate on finishing his new home and improving his farm estate. He also enjoyed speedboat racing on the Connecticut River with his two very fast Indian motorboats. Below, in 1944, he relaxes in his home with his favorite pet, Scotch collie Oscar. (Above, FoFAH; below, WMSH.)

In 1914, Gilbert Heublein, a Hartford spirits merchant, restaurateur, and hotelier (and distributor of A.1. steak sauce), constructed this 165-foot-tall summer house on Talcott Mountain in Simsbury, Connecticut. Modeled after Bavarian tower castles, Heublein Tower is undoubtedly the tallest historic house overlooking the Connecticut River Valley. The steel-framed structure, designed by Hartford architects Smith & Bassette, had 20 windows on four sides of the sixth-floor living room (below), reached by one of the valley's earliest residential elevators. It afforded spectacular views of the valley. Under the ownership of the *Hartford Times* newspaper, beginning in 1943, the room was the scene of many important visits, including in 1950, when Dwight Eisenhower was asked here to run for president. Threatened by residential development, the state purchased 557 acres of the mountain in 1966 and restored this unique home. (Both, FoHT.)

Five

RIVER GENTRY

Nineteenth-century Connecticut River traders, farmers, shipbuilders, and manufacturers created significant family fortunes, which were invested by subsequent generations in grand country estates in the valley. Castles, hilltop villas, and model farms (most often serving as second homes), or a combination of these types, were constructed. Before 1920, without federal income and estate taxes (along with low staffing and maintenance costs), investment in grandly scaled houses was possible. These dominated the prime sites of the valley's landscape.

Earlier, families benefitting from river commerce sought pastoral retreats in suburban enclaves and country seats, typically situated at a distance from noisy mills, shipyards, and wharves. These homes, designed in the early revival styles—Grecian, Gothic, and Italianate—were ideally set in landscapes that followed English precedents for picturesque wildness combined with garden-esque arrangements of formal gardens and specimen plantings. George Atwater's 300-acre Rockrimmon estate north of Springfield, Massachusetts, with a Richard Upjohn–designed mansion surrounded by 15,000 trees of more than 30 varieties, was typical. Others, such as Richard Alsop IV's Regency-style house on High Street in Middletown, Connecticut (built 1840), were unique manifestations of their owners' sophisticated aspirations.

Post–Civil War Gilded Age industrialists and elite families assembled even larger landholdings, consolidating abandoned farmland or upland woodlots and, with the aid of nationally recognized architects and landscape architects, created extravagant estates. These estates included mansion houses in all of the later architectural revival styles with servant outbuildings, greenhouses, vast barns, and ornamental garden follies. Structures were connected by parterred or walled gardens, nature walks, orchards, and fenced pasturelands laid out with an eye for scenic vistas over the river and valley. Working farms and dairies provided produce both for sale to local markets and to be sent to winter homes back in Boston, New York, Springfield, and Hartford. Prize-winning cattle herds and poultry, scientifically raised using the latest techniques and equipment, assuaged the competitive egos of this new generation of gentlemen farmers who vied for the best of breeds.

In the latter half of the 20th century, many of the river's grand estates were subdivided for residential developments or sold to religious orders or schools. Vestiges of some of these estates have remained to anchor large public parks or preserves now enjoyed by many.

Daniel Wadsworth of Hartford, Connecticut, was the son of Jeremiah Wadsworth, merchant entrepreneur, commissary general during the Revolutionary War, and perhaps the state's wealthiest man. Daniel fashioned a 250-acre estate and working farm, Monte Video ("mountain view"), atop Talcott Mountain near Hartford. The house that he designed and built in 1809 (above) was New England's earliest in the Gothic Revival style. It overlooked a spring-fed lake and enjoyed unparalleled panoptic views over the Connecticut and Farmington River valleys (below). In 1810, Wadsworth erected the unique 55-foot-tall, battlemented wooden tower from which the invited public could take in 360-degree views. Artists and travel writers also came from afar to admire the famous country seat and "pleasure grounds." Philanthropist and patron of artists Daniel Wadsworth in 1844 established Hartford's Wadsworth Atheneum, considered to be America's first public museum. (Above, FoHT; below, AM.)

While Col. Jeremiah Taylor had a tavern adjacent to the shipyard on the Connecticut River at Middle Haddam, Connecticut, to escape the bustling riverfront, he moved to The Hill (above left), built in 1795. It was located on Colchester Road in Chatham (now Portland) looking down over Middle Haddam Landing. Jeremiah and Lucy's son Charles Gustavus "Gusta" Taylor inherited The Hill and, between 1856 and 1861, added the Italianate-style three-story tower (above right) to accommodate his twin brother Henry's family. Living in New York City, the two families lived here for portions of each summer and fall. On what came to be known as Taylor Hill, they enjoyed the cool breezes and the dramatic view over the Connecticut River (below in 1890), where it turns to flow south to Long Island Sound. (Above left, PTP; above right, MHL. Below, PTP.)

Jeremiah and Lucy Taylor's eldest son, Knowles, built his summer home next to The Hill in about 1820 (above left). Knowles, a New York City wool merchant, lost his wealth (and this house) to his brother Jeremiah as the first president of the Long Island Railroad when it failed, thus dashing his dream to connect Brooklyn with Long Island's Montauk Point, where he had envisioned constructing a transatlantic seaport. In 1906, his nephew Henry Osborn Taylor and his wife, Julia Isham Taylor, moved Knowles House with teams of oxen a few hundred yards to the west (above right in about 1915) to enjoy better Connecticut River views. Soon thereafter, Henry entertained his brothers on the terrace overlooking the river, as seen below; from left to right are Frank Taylor, who took The Hill; Henry; Howard Taylor; and Charlie Taylor. (Above left, AM; above right, MHL. Below, PTP.)

At Knowles House, Henry and Julia Taylor created a country estate including guest houses, caretaker cottages, gardens, a tennis court, and woodland walks, most of which Julia designed. Henry, a scholar specializing in ancient and medieval studies, and Julia (inset) hosted "Philosopher's Weekends" in October from 1924 to 1939. Photographed in front of the guest house are weekend intellectuals, from left to right, Henry; William Morton Wheeler, Harvard entomologist; Alfred North Whitehead, English mathematician and philosopher; and Lawrence J. Henderson, Harvard professor of biological chemistry. (PTP.)

Meanwhile, Henry's brother Howard Taylor was busy entertaining out-of-town guests at his nearby summer estate, St. Clements, constructed 1900–1903 on a high bluff with sweeping views of the river where it turns south. Howard, a successful corporate attorney in New York City, had reserved the best Taylor family land, straddling Portland and Cobalt, Connecticut, for his estate. (PTP.)

St. Clements was named after the patron saint of sailors and modeled after Norman architecture that Howard and his wife, Gertrude Taylor, had seen in France. It was planned by New York architect Algernon Sidney Bell. The mile-long driveway (above in *Architectural Record* magazine in 1908) wound downhill through varied landscapes including a polo field, designed by "Garden Artist" Charles Wellford Leavitt. It ended at an allée of horse chestnut trees passing through the porte cochére, which then opened into the courtyard (below) that overlooked the river. Better vistas up and down the river were had from the four-story tower that punctuated the 193-foot-long house. Materials employed were local stone, stained chestnut, and cypress shake roof shingles. In 1902, the newspapers reported that the estate would "surpass anything of the kind from Hartford to the Sound." (Both, PTP.)

Designed for entertaining, "the Big Room" (above) was the main living and dining hall at St. Clements, reportedly modeled after the refectory of an old Norman inn. Below left in 1905, Howard Taylor pauses at a window of the Big Room with daughter Eleanor and son Murray. Below right, getting ready for a swim in the Connecticut River from the private dock at the base of the estate's bluff in 1904, Taylor's wife, Gertrude Murray Taylor, prepares to remove her clothing. St. Clements, when later occupied by Howard's son Murray, was frequently the site of parties for visiting celebrities, including actors Donald Cook, Joan Bennett, and Jane Wyatt, sculptor Paul Manship, novelist Alice Duer Miller, guitarist Carlos Montoya, and entertainer Gypsy Rose Lee. St. Clements is now a banquet and conference center. (All, PTP.)

Zebulon Stiles Ely (above left), a retired coffee and sugar importer from New York, returned to ancestral land in Lyme, Connecticut, where, in 1873, he constructed his granite-walled country home in the French mansard style with a Stick-style porte cochére (above right). From the ponderous cupola with balconies, Ely's family could have enjoyed a panoramic view from the high elevation of Lord Hill over Lord's Cove west to the Connecticut River. The view would have encompassed much of Zebulon's ancestor Englishman Richard Ely's 3,000-acre plantation (below) that included Six Mile Island in the river, exclusive rights to the Ely's landing and ferry, with crossing over to Essex, and the Ely Meadow, where, in the 18th century, farming proprietors purchased plots for the harvesting of salt hay and grazing land for their livestock. (Above left, AM; above right, LPH&LHA. Below, LHSA@FGM.)

In 1886, Edward and Harriet "Hattie" Brainerd constructed this Queen Anne–style home directly overlooking the Connecticut River in Middle Haddam, Connecticut. It was adjacent to the home of her father, steamboat captain Edward Simpson. The Brainerds lived in Chicago, spending summers and autumns here. Edward Brainerd, whose ancestors were closely connected with quarry operations in the valley, was a cut stone dealer with marble and granite quarries in Vermont, New York, and Joliet, Illinois, where he was accused by competitors of using prison labor to cut his stone. He was bankrupt by 1898. The Brainerds also built the dock house seen below, beyond the house, in about 1890. The Knowles Landing section of Middle Haddam, no longer a vibrant shipbuilding center, was still a steamboat stop, where the steamers brought freight and New York tourists to the surrounding picturesque villages. (Both, MHL.)

Another steamboat stop was at the Rock Landing boardinghouse in Haddam Neck, Connecticut. Originally the 1813 home of Dudley Brainerd, with a store on the lowest level, by 1870, it was an inn operated by Charles and Selina Russell, who added the mansard-roofed third floor and porches overlooking the river. The landing served the burgeoning steamboat traffic, trading fish and lumber for weekend tourists from New York. (Left, MHL; right, AM.)

Looking out over Eustacia Island, the landing and shipyard on Kirtland's Rock at Deep River, Connecticut, was an earlier home significantly overhauled in the prevailing Italianate style by Stillman Tiley about 1854 to accommodate 20 steamboat tourist guests in what he called the Wahginnicut House. This 1878 view is by George Bradford Brainerd, a Haddam, Connecticut, native who extensively photographed lower valley scenery and inhabitants. (BM/BPL, BC.)

Woodside was Sherman Paris's name for his six-acre Charlestown, New Hampshire, estate not far from the Connecticut River (above). The core of the main house was the Georgian-style 1774 Simeon Olcott House, which dominated the south end of Main Street. After purchasing the estate in 1867, Paris overhauled the house in the latest Victorian fashion. He added the central turreted tower with a private chapel at the center front, a large three-story tower addition to the south side, new windows, and elaborately detailed woodwork throughout. A new stable in the French mansard style popular in the 1870s, a tool house, icehouse, greenhouse, servant's cottages, and a church were also added by Paris—all commemorated in the engraved view below. Flower gardens and a lily pond enhanced the compound, which was widely acclaimed in the valley. (Both, CHS.)

Sherman Paris (above, left) poses on the front lawn of his home with, from left to right, Rev. Paul Rogers Fish, his daughter Eugenie Paris, and friend Nellie Painter. Paris was a manufacturer of barrel staves, an inventor of distillery machinery, and a part owner of Paris, Allen & Company of New York, a wholesale liquor distiller and importer of spirits. At one time, he had a large stake in distributing Old Crow and Hermitage whiskeys, then Kentucky's preeminent bourbons. The showstopper on his estate was the grandly scaled and intricately detailed summer pavilion (left), which he commissioned from German architect Theodore Karls of Chicago. The exotic pavilion, added to the gardens in 1873, was the talk of the upper valley. The mansard-roofed design was composed of terra-cotta architectural details likely manufactured in Chicago. (Both, CHS.)

The house at Woodside may be the valley's most transmogrified structure as successive owners remodeled it according to the latest architectural trends. Simeon Olcott, chief justice of New Hampshire's supreme court, constructed the original Georgian mansion. Its flanking wings engulfing an older house made a grandiose statement in the upper valley befitting its owner's status. Soon after 1925, Sherman Paris's "Victorianized" house (above) was returned mostly to its original appearance, but with Colonial Revival touches, when Katherine Colvin Budd took possession. Budd removed Paris's towers and added the portico with columns salvaged from a local church (below). Renamed Maxstoke, she envisioned it could be the summer site of New York's Whitney Studio Club, and with sculptor Gertrude Vanderbilt Whitney and museum director Juliana Force, an arts colony briefly flourished here in 1927 when painters Edward Hopper and Charles Sheeler exhibited their latest work in its salons. (Both, CHS.)

Everett Hosmer Barney, who made his fortune patenting and manufacturing clamp-on ice skates, constructed Pecousic Villa (built 1883–1885) atop Long Hill, commanding an enviable view over the Connecticut River and Springfield, Massachusetts. Named after the nearby brook that flowed into the river, the house was designed by local architects Richmond & Seabury in a combination of Queen Anne and Romanesque Revival styles, influenced by Boston architect H.H. Richardson's domestic designs. The brick construction with Longmeadow brownstone trim was enhanced with decorative terra-cotta and panels of seashells that Barney had collected in Florida. Two 62-foot-tall lookout towers were topped with gilded copper. Patrick Beston was the mason, while Edwin Shattuck carved the elaborate finish carpentry, seen below in the main stairwell with its unusual fireplace tucked below the stairs. (Both, WMSH.)

Starting in 1912, Everett Hosmer Barney added extensive porches and closed loggias around his Springfield riverfront house (above). Barney was undoubtedly imagining how Springfield citizens might better enjoy the sweeping views of the Connecticut River, for he had willed his house and grounds to the city in 1890, retaining life tenancy. He also laid out the grounds of his park-like 178-acre estate with exotic ornamental plants from all over the world. Harnessing the Pecousic River's water flow, he created ponds and streams (seen below around 1905), establishing unique aquatic gardens filled with Egyptian lotus flowers and intersected by walking and carriage paths. His mansion and carriage house can be seen at upper right. (Above, AM; below, LOC.)

Everett Hosmer Barney was an inveterate tinkerer. Besides ice and roller skates, he invented a breech-loading shotgun, a perforation machine, and a saluting canon for mounting on boat decks. From his front lawn, he fired the canon whenever a recreational steamboat passed by. Barney loved living on the Connecticut River and enjoyed all water sports and activities. Here, he demonstrates his design for a lifesaving water and ice pontoon sled (left) with Pecousic Villa visible above the river. Until almost the end of his life, he enjoyed demonstrating his skates (right).

Everett Hosmer Barney's gift of his estate to Springfield extended the adjacent 65-acre Forest Park to the Connecticut River's bank. Famous landscape architect Frederick Law Olmsted designed the consolidated parkland, now the largest municipal park on the river. Since 1921, the Barney estate was enjoyed for picnics and viewing river races. The house was repurposed for a museum of Springfield's industrial arts and natural history, attracting 40,000 visitors a year by the 1950s. (WMSH.)

Barney also owned the first gasoline-powered launch seen on the river (left) and designed and built rigged canoes (known as Pecowsic canoes), winning many races on the river, sailing them himself (right). (All, AM.)

In 1892, Everett Hosmer Barney constructed this family mausoleum designed by Francis Richmond, including Italian marble sphinxes and a river-viewing loggia above. This site on Laurel Hill was to have been the location for his son's home, but George Barney died of a lung ailment in 1889. The mausoleum and the original carriage house remain, but Pecousic Villa was demolished in 1959 with the construction of Interstate Highway 91. (LHS.)

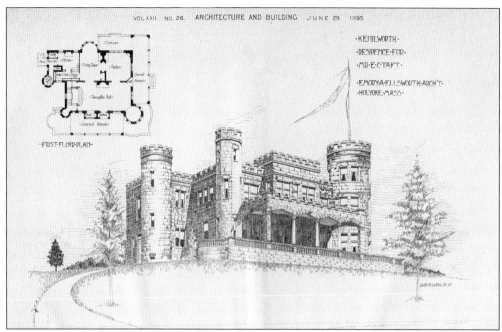

·KENILWORTH·
·RESIDENCE·FOR·
·MR·E·C·TAFT·

·EMORY·A·ELLSWORTH·ARCH'T·
·HOLYOKE·MASS·

·FIRST·FLOOR·PLAN·

In 1895, Edward Taft, a paper mill owner, constructed this castle-like summer home he called Kenilworth (after Walter Scott's novel) in Northampton (now Holyoke), Massachusetts. The triple-towered Gothic Revival house was designed by Holyoke architect and civil engineer Emory A. Ellsworth. His rendering of the new house appeared in *Architecture and Building* (above), modeled after William Gladstone's Hawarden Castle. A relatively modest-sized home (below), the fascinated public assumed it was much grander in scale. Taft's son-in-law William Flagg, who subsequently lived here, when asked how he got from one end of the "mansion" to the other, quipped, "Well, we catch the boat coming up the river at nine o'clock at night, and when we get off at nine o'clock the next morning, we're at the other end of the house." (Above, HPL/HHR; below, WMA.)

Edward Taft's Kenilworth was a picturesque landmark that sat above an artificially created knoll and commanded a view over the Connecticut River (seen above in 1899). At the water's edge is the Holyoke Canoe Club's boathouse. The Summit House Hotel (built 1897) is atop Mount Tom in the distance. On his riverfront estate, Taft raised prize poultry and pursued his hobby as an early short-wave radio enthusiast. From this height, he boasted that he was able to dial in 6,500 stations from around the world. Taft filled the house's interiors, designed like a hunting lodge, with art and furnishings collected traveling the world (as seen below in the entrance hall). The showplace was demolished in 1959; many of its unique architectural elements were sold for repurposing in area restaurants. (Above, HPL/VSDC; below, AM.)

The most ambitiously pretentious house constructed along the Connecticut River, Chalet Schell was completed in 1903. Its four circular towers dominated the skyline of the small farming village of Northfield, Massachusetts (above around 1913). It was built by New Yorker Francis Schell and designed by New York architect Bruce Price. While modeled after the chateaus of France's Loire River Valley, it more specifically resembled a scaled-down version of the Hotel Chateau Frontenac (built 1893) that overlooked the St. Lawrence River and old Quebec City (also designed by Price). From its commanding site, the Schells enjoyed views over the river valley to Vermont's Green Mountain and New Hampshire's White Mountain ranges. The mansion later served as a guesthouse and religious conference center for the nearby Northfield Inn. In the c. 1930 image below, conference attendees pose on the front steps of the chateau. (Both, NMHA.)

The original Schell estate included 125 acres sloping down to the river and featured an artificial lagoon and Italian gardens defined by columnar cypress trees, and overlooked from a covered terrace on the south side (above). Childless Francis and Mary Schell occupied Birnam House, as they named it, during summers only. The mansion had over 100 rooms, including 36 bedrooms and 23 bathrooms, a private chapel, elevator, and double spiral stairs. It was lavishly decorated in a style consistent with the high-society mansions of Newport, Rhode Island. Its Gold Room (below in 1931) was enjoyed by many summer visitors to the Northfield Inn as the setting for concerts, teas, and card parties. The grand house was demolished in 1963 but is remembered fondly by Northfield Mount Hermon school students as the venue, since 1939, for their senior prom, known as The Chat. (Both, NMHA.)

Dominating Longmeadow, Massachusetts's, historic town green is the Brewer-Young Mansion, a grand Southern Colonial–style house. In 1906, Edward and Corrinne Brewer transformed the shingled Colonial Revival–style Wolcott House (built in 1884), adding the portico, side bays, porte cochère, and loggias. Dark-stained shingles were replaced with white clapboard and classical trim, all of which required a crew of six men to paint white (seen above in 1911). Edward Brewer was a businessman and hotelier and also a politician and gentleman farmer. In the 1908 image below, two years after the construction of his house, he rests with a grandchild on his loggia. Paesiello Emerson, who took up photography after age 70, took these and many other excellent photographs of structures and life in central Massachusetts. (Both, LHS.)

The 18-acre Brewer-Young estate, part in farmland, ran from Longmeadow Street down to the Connecticut River (seen above in 1908). From 1921 to 1960, widow Mary Ida Young owned the Brewer property, which she named Meadowview Farms. Mary and Wilbur Young, from Springfield, invented Absorbine muscle liniment for horses in 1892 and Absorbine Jr. for humans in 1903. Mary Ida Young's estate was the setting for many of Longmeadow's social events, overseen by fashionable Young with her borzois (below). She extensively landscaped Brewer's farmland with formal gardens and fountains, but much of the riverfront property was eventually taken by eminent domain for the construction of Interstate Highway 91. In 2018, the Longmeadow Historic Preservation Partners saved the Brewer-Young Mansion from destruction and oversaw a prize-winning restoration of the landmark, now serving as professional offices. (Above, LHS; below, WMSH.)

The eccentric Col. Clarence Seymour Wadsworth and his wife, Katharine, constructed their 20,000-square-foot Long Hill mansion in Middletown, Connecticut, from 1909 to 1917. The Classical Revival design, advanced for its time with fireproof construction of reinforced concrete, was by Hoppin & Koen architects of New York City, known for Gilded Age mansions. Sitework started in 1900, and the 750-acre estate developed over 22 years in consultation with landscape architects Olmsted Brothers. Wadsworth was a conservationist of open spaces and an ardent tree lover. He oversaw the reforestation of this once-open orchard and farmland (seen above in 1913). The mansion's south side (below) was Palladian in design, with Italian gardens that Katharine laid out with landscape architect Charles Leavitt. In 1935, Wadsworth formed the Rockfall Corporation, which later donated 267 acres to the state, now the Wadsworth Falls State Park. (Both, TWMLH.)

Banker and politician John Wingate Weeks built his summer lodge in 1912 at the summit of his 420-acre estate atop Mount Prospect near Lancaster, New Hampshire. The Weeks Estate is typical of grand New Hampshire retreats constructed by wealthy families who amalgamated failing farms and hilly uplands in the early 20th century. Weeks's Craftsman-style house was constructed of fieldstone, half-timbered stucco, and undulating terra-cotta roof tiles. An 87-foot-tall water tower afforded panoramic vistas of the river valley below. Below, guests including Pres. Warren Harding attempt a round of golf on the somewhat rugged course around the tower. US senator Weeks authored the Weeks Act of 1911, leading to the decline of clear-cutting and strip mining that plagued the upper valley. He was known as the "Father of the Eastern National Forests." (Both, LPC/BPL.)

The Upham family built a number of country homes on Jarvis Hill, which dominated a bend in the Connecticut River at West Claremont, New Hampshire. Patriarch James Phineas Upham was a manufacturer of engine lathes, planers, saws, mowing machines, and ploughs, but especially turbine water wheels. In 1869, he founded the family business, Sullivan Machinery Company, specializing in the manufacture of mining and quarrying equipment. He purchased the Dove Farm and, surely influenced by the writings of landscape architect A.J. Downing, built this board and batten–style home in 1850. The 213-acre gentleman's farm (which he named Uplands) included fruit orchards, Jersey cattle, and merino and Southdown sheep. The farm's spectacular view of the river and Mount Ascutney to the north was painted by Albert Bierstadt in 1862 (below), with Upham's cows and sheep in the foreground. (Above, AM; below, FMtToR.)

James Phineas Upham's oldest son, James Duncan Upham, who had a village house in Claremont, New Hampshire, where he oversaw the family business started by his father, built his summer home on his father's estate, Uplands. Above around 1915, Upham and his family set out for a drive from the simple stone and shingled house, which he dubbed By-The-Connecticut. Like his father, he sited his home to take in the view of Mount Ascutney and the Green Mountains. In the photograph below, similar to the Bierstadt painting on the previous page, he enjoys the river view. (Above, SSC; below, HNE.)

In 1912, Boston attorney George Baxter Upham, James Phineas Upham's second son, constructed his summer place at the highest elevation of Uplands in Claremont, New Hampshire. George Upham, interested in Boston's development, was considered the "Father of the Boston Subway." He also lobbied for building height restrictions and one-way streets. His classically grand manor house, named Upland Court, was enhanced with Arts and Crafts touches throughout. Arcaded porches, balconies, bay windows, and garden pavilions graciously integrated exterior and interior spaces. The north side (above), overlooking the river, features a monumental porch. The south side (below) was formally organized with a center entrance, automobile court, and geometric gardens. Boston architects Warren and Smith designed the mansion in brick and stucco with antique tiles embedded in walls, documented by Maureen Meister in *Architecture and the Arts and Crafts Movement in Boston*. (Both, HNE.)

Life at Kent Place in Suffield, Connecticut, was extensively photographed in 1901. The original house, constructed by Benajah Kent 100 years prior, was enlarged in 1891 to incorporate 35 rooms on 206 acres by his grandson Sidney A. Kent to serve as a summer home (above). Kent, a Suffield native, made his fortune in Chicago meatpacking and various other speculative businesses involving furs, lumber, land, and gas, but was perhaps best known as a champion of the eight-hour workday. He contributed much to the University of Chicago, including the Kent Chemical Laboratory building, and in Suffield, he funded a library in 1899 in his family's name. His country house expansion in the Colonial Revival style included deep, shady porches on the north side (below). These outdoor rooms, popular at the time, were furnished with fancy fringed hammocks, rattan chaises, and rockers. (Both, KML.)

William J. Wilgus built Iridge (named after an ancestral estate in England) in 1923–1924 in Weathersfield, Vermont (above, architect's rendering). After a long search for Connecticut River frontage, Wilgus selected this site with panoramic views over the river and toward Mount Ascutney to the north. Wilgus was a distinguished civil engineer for many railroads, best remembered as designing the masterful concept for New York's Grand Central Station, with its "air rights" development above two levels of railroad tracks. As Colonel Wilgus, he directed troop transportation during World War I. Wilgus, pictured below in 1929 with his dog Larry, retired to the Georgian Revival–style house with white-painted brick designed by New York architect Charles May and landscaping by society landscape architect Clarence Fowler. In 1933, Wilgus donated over 100 riverside acres to Vermont, now Wilgus State Park. (Both, VHS.)

Six

RIVER MASTERS

Masters of their crafts—authors, poets, playwrights, journalists, actors, painters, illustrators, sculptors, photographers, intellectuals and scientists, architects, engineers, and builders—all inhabited the Connecticut River Valley. Scenic valley towns, such as Cornish, New Hampshire, and Old Lyme, Connecticut, had active colonies of artists and their admirers. Hartford's Nook Farm neighborhood was home to many important authors of the late 19th century. Summer theaters attracted playwrights, actors, and visitors to the "boards." Many admirers of the valley's beauty stayed. Their homes were designed by creative architects and talented builders. Intrepid photographers captured it all.

The upper river valley was especially conducive to reclusive writers. Emily Dickinson lived in Amherst, Massachusetts, while Edward Bellamy's home can be seen in Chicopee Falls, Massachusetts. J.D. Salinger (author of *The Catcher in the Rye*, published in 1951) lived in Cornish, New Hampshire. Russian dissident and author Aleksandr Solzhenitsyn, after writing *The Gulag Archipelago*, published in 1973, lost his Soviet citizenship and fled to Cavendish, Vermont, where he lived until 1994. The valley's colleges and universities attracted talented scholars, including the author William Manchester, whose Mid-century modern house in Middletown, Connecticut, was known as "the house that Jack [Kennedy] built." Manchester used payments he received from *Look* magazine, which had serialized his bestselling book, *Death of a President*. Local citizens zealously guarded the privacy of these internationally respected authors.

Artists found the valley's landscapes inspirational and the seclusion of its villages restorative, yet they could remain close to New York and Boston art markets. Regionalist printmaker Thomas W. Nason and Impressionist painters James Goodwin McManus and Carleton and Guy Wiggins had homes and studios on Joshuatown Road in Lyme, Connecticut. Robert Childress of Old Saybrook, Connecticut, illustrated the *Tom, Dick, and Jane* books using his own family and friends as models. The childhood home of Dr. Seuss (Theodore Geisel) remains in Springfield, Massachusetts.

The valley also was the home of America's first playwright, Royall Tyler (Brattleboro, Vermont). Important scientists lived here as well. Mary Ann Booth of Longmeadow, Massachusetts, was a pioneering photomicroscopist who, in the early 20th century, won medals at science conferences for her contributions leading to the final elimination of bubonic plague.

George C. Fisk.

THE valued president is he
    Of a great Springfield industry.
  On many a track the Wason car
  Carries his reputation far.
Of ample tastes, his phonograph
Suffices for an evening's laugh.
    His home and farm he loves the best,
    And with them he feels amply blest.

Josiah Gilbert Holland grew up in river valley towns, and after various careers, settled in Springfield, Massachusetts, with native Elizabeth Chapin. There, he took up writing, assisting editor Samuel Bowles on his influential newspaper, the *Springfield Daily Republican*. Holland's historical fiction, novels, poetry, and essays, while sentimentally moralistic, brought him national acclaim in the 1850s. With financial success, he built Brightwood (above) in 1863 on a 150-foot bluff overlooking the Connecticut River, designed by architect Leopold Eidlitz in the ornamental Swiss-chalet style. Here, Holland wrote the first best-selling biography of Abraham Lincoln. Generations of the Fisk family later occupied the estate. George Fisk, president of Wason Manufacturing, built railway coaches and streetcars in his new plant nearby. But, per the caricature at left, "His home and farm he loves the best / And with them he feels amply blest." (Both, WMSH.)

Writer George Washington Cable called the Dutch Colonial–style home he built in 1892 in Northampton, Massachusetts, Tarryawhile. Cable (above inset and below right) had been a well-established novelist of New Orleans's Creole society, considered by many to be the first modern Southern writer. His later writing, produced in his backyard studio in Northampton (below left), was more didactic than artistic, as he became interested in social activist causes such as prison reform, civil rights, and racial equality. Cable invited famous authors, including speaking tour partner Mark Twain, James M. Barrie, and Arthur Conan Doyle, to plant "souvenir" trees along the street he called Dryads Green (after New Orleans' Dryad Street). Cable was also instrumental in establishing Home Culture Clubs in Northampton, which promoted education and gardening for working adults. (Above, FLib; inset, AM. Below left, AM; below right, SAAM.)

Journalist, travel writer, and essayist Charles Dudley Warner earned national recognition with his book *My Summer in a Garden* (published in 1870) but is best remembered as Mark Twain's co-author of *The Gilded Age: A Tale of Today* (1873). The book gave the post–Civil War era a name that stuck. Warner was also known for his sassy quips, such as "Everybody complains about the weather, but nobody does anything about it." One of the early inhabitants of the Nook Farm neighborhood, the prestigious enclave of the intelligentsia in Hartford, Connecticut, Warner later moved into this house there in 1884. It was built by his brother George in 1873 and designed by New York architect Edward Tuckerman Potter. Connecticut Valley photographer Clifton Johnson captured Charles Dudley Warner at his home (below)—apt visual representations of the writer who preferred novels of nostalgic domesticity. (Above, CTHS; below, JLib.)

Nook Farm's 140 acres along the Park River on the west side of Hartford, Connecticut, were developed for an upscale residential subdivision in the mid-19th century. Its bucolic setting was close to the thriving city that was a center of manufacturing, insurance, and publishing. The development attracted community leaders, intellectuals, authors, and social activists, many of whom were related by marriage. Here, they built fashionable homes set within a park-like landscape with interconnecting paths and drives. In 1864, Harriet Beecher Stowe built her second Hartford home here, a more modest cottage (above). Harriet (below) and her husband, Rev. Calvin Stowe, were abolitionists. She was the author of the 19th century's bestselling and highly influential novel *Uncle Tom's Cabin; or, Life Among the Lowly* (published in 1852). Another bestselling author, Mark Twain, was her neighbor. His house is visible in the distance above. (Both, HBSC.)

Missourian Samuel Clemens (above inset), better known as Mark Twain, was attracted to Hartford, Connecticut, by its publishing, printing, and book production industries when his first book, *The Innocents Abroad* (1869) was published there by American Publishing. Here, in 1874, he constructed a 19-room mansion (above) in the Nook Farm neighborhood, close by the homes of other literary stars, such as Charles Dudley Warner and Harriet Beecher Stowe. It was his home for 17 years, where he wrote large portions of some of America's most important books, including *The Adventures of Tom Sawyer* (1876) and *Adventures of Huckleberry Finn* (1884), among others. Below, in 1886, he poses on the veranda with his wife, Livy, and daughters (from left to right) Susy, Jean, and Clara. *Forbes Magazine* named the Mark Twain House the "best museum house in America." (Above, LOC; below, BRB&ML.)

Mark Twain employed architect Edward Tuckerman Potter to design his home. The house is a Ruskinian High Gothic–style tour-de-force composition of picturesque roofline gables, dormers, balconies, and porches intricately finished with Windsor brick, brownstone, and ornately carved wood elements. The dramatic porte cochère (above left) greeted guests at the front door. The interior rooms (entrance hall, above right) were decorated in stunning Aesthetic-style finishes by Louis Comfort Tiffany. (LOC.)

In 1884, attorney Franklin Chamberlain and his wife, Mary Porter Chamberlain, employed New York architect Francis H. Kimball to design this magnificent Queen Anne–style home (with enchanting Arts and Crafts elements) in Hartford, Connecticut. A later owner of the house was Katharine Seymour Day. She was a public health advocate and historic preservationist largely responsible for saving the neighboring Mark Twain and Harriet Beecher Stowe Houses. (LOC.)

Many are surprised to learn that the popular Indian-born English author Rudyard Kipling built a home in Dummerston, near Brattleboro, Vermont (after marrying Vermont native Caroline Balestier). The green-stained Shingle-style, ship-like home was set on 11 acres with views across the valley to Mount Monadnock. Its design by New York architect Henry Rutgers Marshall had strong hints of Anglo-Indian bungalow architecture and was named Naulakha ("a thing of great value" in Hindi). The author's time here, from 1893 to 1896, was productive and peaceful. Kipling, seen at left in his writing study, wrote his *Jungle Book* duology (published in 1894 and 1895) and *Captains Courageous* (1896) while living in Vermont, leading to him being awarded the Nobel Prize for Literature in 1907. Kipling was very fond of the river valley. Here, he hosted Arthur Conan Doyle, author of the Sherlock Holmes stories. (Both, LTUSA.)

In 1899, bestselling novelist Winston Churchill (1871–1947) completed his summer home, Harlakenden, in Cornish, New Hampshire. Named for his wife, Mabel Harlakenden Hall, a prominent suffragist, the Georgian Revival house was designed by New York architect Charles Platt, who also summered in Cornish and designed important homes there. Harlakenden was known as "the Summer Capitol" when leased by Pres. Woodrow Wilson from 1913 to 1915 as a seasonal getaway from Washington. (AM.)

The Oaks was artist Maxfield Parrish's name for his 45-acre estate in Plainfield, New Hampshire, which included the home and studio he designed, from 1898 until his death in 1966. The setting, with an ethereal view over the valley to Mount Ascutney, often supplied him with inspiration for his work, especially his iconic painting *Daybreak* (1922), the most reproduced image in American art history. (JLib; inset, LOC.)

Aspet is what prominent New York sculptor of public monuments Augustus Saint-Gaudens called his home (above) in Cornish, New Hampshire. After visiting the upper valley in 1885, Saint-Gaudens stayed, and in 1894 purchased the house known locally as "Huggins' Folly." He and his wife, Augusta, renovated the house, adding distinctive piazzas to each end from which to enjoy views over the valley. They also continuously relandscaped its 150-acre grounds, creating a sculpted landscape. Saint-Gaudens's residency in Cornish was largely responsible for attracting artists, writers, musicians, architects, and landscape architects to what came to be the renowned Cornish Art Colony. Below, he is seen peering out from the pergola of his sculpture studio building, completed in 1904 (George Fletcher Babb, architect). The National Park Service acquired the site in 1965, and it is now the Saint-Gaudens National Historical Park. (Both, DCL/RSC.)

In 1920, Evelyn Longman began working in a newly constructed studio in Windsor, Connecticut (above), designed in the Arts and Crafts style by architect Richard Henry Dana. She had moved her thriving art career from New York City to join her spouse, Nathaniel Batchelder, headmaster of the Loomis School, whom she met while sculpting a memorial for his first wife, Gwendolen. Longman sculpted many important private commissions and public monuments over three decades in this studio (humorously called "Chiselhurst-on-Farmington" after the local river that feeds the Connecticut River nearby). These commissions included Hartford's Spanish-American War Memorial of 1927; below, she is seen working on the central figure. An apartment in the studio housed visitors who assisted Longman. (Both photographs from the collection of the Loomis Chaffee Archives, Loomis Chaffee School; above, White Studio; below, Broderick, Windsor.)

In 1817, William Noyes Jr. constructed this late Georgian-style home (above) on the bank of the Lieutenant River near its confluence with the Connecticut River in Old Lyme, Connecticut. Packet shipmaster Robert Griswold purchased it in 1841. His daughter Florence Griswold inherited the house along with his outstanding debts. After operating a ladies' school here, Florence, encouraged by a boarder, the painter Henry Ward Ranger (who sought a country base for like-minded painters of the tonalist school), opened the house in 1900 to his artist friends. Willard Metcalf's painting *May Night* (left) of 1906 depicted "Miss Florence" approaching the "Holy House." When the work quickly sold for $3,000, it brought attention to the Old Lyme colony. Established painters, art students, and collectors swarmed the village; the Lyme School of Art was born. (Above, LHSA@FGM; left, NGA.)

For 30 years, Florence Griswold's house served as the center of a significant seasonal artist's colony. An estimated 200 painters came to the town and environs to record in paint and pastels, *en plein air*, the beauty and historic character of the lower valley's landscapes. The house is considered the birthplace of the American school of Impressionism after painter Childe Hassam's influence. Griswold (above) was the center of the colony; her artists gratefully decorated the walls of her boardinghouse with paintings that humorously chronicled their interactions. The painted panels themselves became tourist attractions. At lunch on the side porch, the artists would gather for raucous conversation; the men's group was dubbed the Hot Air Club (below in 1905). The house, restored to its 1910 appearance, is a national historic landmark and is now the center of the Florence Griswold Museum campus. (Both, LHSA@FGM.)

Boxwood was the name given to Richard Griswold Jr.'s father's late Federal-style home (above around 1885) in Old Lyme, Connecticut, when enlarged by Richard Jr. for his family of eight children in 1841. Griswold extensively re-landscaped the 20-acre farm estate. In 1891, his wife, Rosa Brown Griswold, established the Boxwood School for Girls here when the third floor was added. By 1905, Boxwood Manor became the summer boarding home and studio venue for visiting artists and their students drawn to the Lyme Art Colony, which originated at nearby Florence Griswold's home. Like so many artists who depicted the blossoming gardens of Old Lyme, painter Charles Vezin centered the house in his work *Gardens at Boxwood*; he can be seen painting it below around 1927. The swanky inn's wraparound veranda, shaded by wisteria, was another oft-painted subject for Lyme artists. (Both, LHSA@FGM.)

Heinz Warneke (above left) was a sculptor in the Modernist style known for his "direct carving" skills. After 1932, he had his country home and studio in the 1738 Daniel Olmsted House (The Mowings) in East Haddam, Connecticut. With his business partner and wife, Jessie, Warneke earned many public and private commissions, including the south portal of the Washington, DC, National Cathedral (1932–1939), Penn State's Nittany Lion (1942), and the eagles that graced Washington, DC's, Social Security Building (above right, around 1945 in East Haddam). Warneke's contemporary, painter and illustrator W. Langdon Kihn (below inset), also lived in East Haddam, moving into his wife Helen Butler's family home there (below), originally the Samuel Emmons Tavern, built about 1690. Kihn was renowned for his portraits of indigenous North Americans and his impressionistic paintings of the lower river valley. (All, EHHS.)

This home in Springfield, Massachusetts, occupied by George and Belle Smith in 1902, was built in 1836, with the mansard roof added later (above). The original owners were historian and diplomat George Bancroft and his wife, Sarah Dwight. Here, Bancroft wrote much of his acclaimed *History of the United States, from the Discovery of the American Continent.* George Smith, a successful carriage manufacturer in New York City, with his wife, Belle (left), were early preeminent art dealers and collectors, traveling the world and establishing a collection of more than 6,000 works. Their collections became the basis for Springfield's George Walter Vincent Smith Art Museum, established in 1896, now at the heart of the city's cultural district. Pictured above is the Smiths' house on Chestnut Street in 1925. At left are George Walter Vincent Smith and Belle Townsley Smith in the 1890s. (Above, The Smiths' House on Chestnut Street, 1925; left, George Walter Vincent Smith and Belle Townsley Smith with Collection Objects, 1890s. Courtesy GWVS Art Museum Archives.)

In 1930, A. Everett "Chick" Austin Jr. (inset above, around 1936) modeled his Palladian-style villa in Hartford, Connecticut (above), after Scamozzi's Villa Ferreti (built in 1596) near Venice, Italy. He brilliantly combined trendsetting modernist aesthetics with European Rococo style in its design and interior decor. Austin, director of the Wadsworth Atheneum Museum in Hartford and an innovative wunderkind, established the city as a center of avant-garde arts. Luminaries of the art world such as Salvador Dali, Le Corbusier, Gertrude Stein, Kurt Weill, Martha Graham, and Virgil Thompson visited the house. It was a stage set for glamorous parties, such as one for the visiting Ballet Russe de Monte Carlo in the living room (below in 1938), with Chick (center) and his wife, Helen Goodwin Austin (foreground in chair), entertained in high style. Austin quipped, "The house is just like me, all facade." (Both, WAMofAA.)

After success as a playwright and producer of farce comedies such as A *Trip to Chinatown* (1891), Charles Hoyt established a summer home in his native Charlestown, New Hampshire. In 1887, he remodeled the 1797 Clark House on Main Street, adding towers, porches, bay windows, parquet flooring, and marble mantlepieces throughout its 19 rooms (above). Thomas Flavin, its master carpenter, was similarly Victorianizing Sherman Paris's house nearby (see pages 105–107). Funnyman Hoyt had a tragic personal life in Charlestown. Actress Flora Welch, his first wife, died in 1893. Actress Caroline Miskel, his second wife, died at childbirth in 1898, also losing their baby. Crushed by his losses, Charles passed in 1900. After his death, the house's caretaker maintained the parlor (below in 1888), where Hoyt had displayed portraits of his wives, memorialized with fresh-cut flowers placed there daily. (Above, CHS; below, SAAM.)

Summer theater troupes rehearsed plays and partied in Charles Hoyt's casino (above) set at the rear of his park-like five-acre estate Clover in Charlestown, New Hampshire. The casino, which he built in 1892, was where he wrote many plays. It included a theater/dance hall, dining room, and a den filled with mismatched furnishings and theater memorabilia. Hoyt (inset above) based many of his Broadway plays' characters, plots, and scenes on Charlestown locals he came to know. Hoyt paraded three Texas longhorns through New York to publicize his play *A Texas Steer* in 1891; the cattle peacefully pose in front of the house's porte cochère (below). He wrote the play for his first wife, actress Flora Walsh, who gazes from the window. Hoyt willed Clover to the Lamb's Club of New York, an acting guild, to be used as a retirement retreat for actors. (Both, CHS.)

Built atop one of the Seven Sister hills of the lower valley, Seventh Sister was the name that actor William Gillette gave to the local fieldstone and steel-framed "castle" he constructed from 1914 to 1926 overlooking the river in East Haddam, Connecticut (above left). Playwright and stage director Gillette (above right) was a Hartford native who made his reputation and fortune adapting the Sherlock Holmes novels of Arthur Conan Doyle for the stage. He also acted the role of Holmes for almost 33 years, crafting the detective's personae as we know it today. The 14,000-square-foot retirement home had the latest technological amenities, including an electrical generator. Stone and hand-hewn southern oak woodwork adorn the interiors (the Great Hall is seen below). Forty-seven different doors with puzzle locks and other ingenious gadgets, imagined by playful Gillette, delight modern-day visitors to the castle. (Both, GCSPA.)

William Gillette's *Aunt Polly* may be the most famous houseboat to ply the Connecticut River's waters. Cruising in the 142-foot vessel (outfitted with a fireplace), Gillette selected the site for his castle, and from it, he directed the five years of its initial construction high above the river (above). After completing construction, he placed the boat on a foundation to serve as a garden house. Gillette's 122-acre estate may be the only one in the valley with a quarter-scale railroad. Train enthusiast Gillette constructed the three-mile narrow-gauge track in 1927 to carry his steam and electric engines. He locomoted guests around the property, affording thrilling views of the river from the gazebo stop at the Ships Stern rock (below left). Below right, Gillette proudly poses before his own "Grand Central Station" that housed his beloved trains. (Both, GCSPA.)

Connecticut valley architect Asher Benjamin constructed this house in 1797 for attorney William Coleman in Greenfield, Massachusetts. Coleman requested Benjamin design and build him a "house worthy of its view" over the Green River Valley. Benjamin promulgated the Federal style throughout the country with his influential builder's guidebooks. This house later served as a store, tavern, girl's school, and a funeral home, as seen here around 1934. (LOC.)

In 1811, master builder Simon Sanborn constructed this house in Springfield, Massachusetts, for James Byers, storekeeper of the Springfield Armory and supplies contractor during the War of 1812. Likely based on a design by architect Asher Benjamin, the groundbreaking house featured parlors across the front and a classical portico distinguished by shaped windows in the pediment. Sanborn went on to design and build many of Springfield's most important homes and buildings. (JLib.)

Henry Bowers's house, built in 1827 in Northampton, Massachusetts (above left), and Samuel Russell's house in Middletown, Connecticut (above right), constructed three years later, were both designed by the important New York architect Ithiel Town. Bowers, from Middletown, was a successful dry goods merchant. Samuel Russell, Bowers's brother-in-law, founded Russell & Company, the most important trading combine in China for much of the 19th century, dealing in teas, silks, and opium. These renderings by Town's partner Alexander Jackson Davis were the only houses to appear in Hinton's *History and Topography of the United States* (1831). These two architectural masterpieces, with their classically correct proportions, had outsized influence in spreading the popularity of the Greek Revival style throughout the country. The Russell House is a designated national historic landmark and remains on the Wesleyan University campus, while the Bowers House (below) was unfortunately razed in 1916. (Above, AM; below, FLib.)

Architect, Ulrich Franzen; *Steel fabricator*: Thames Valley Steel Corp.

Is this New England home too daring for the West?

It stands on the crest of a hill in Connecticut, overlooking the Essex River and Long Island Sound. And a remarkable house it is. The "living" area is an elegant pavilion, 40 ft square, with floor-to-ceiling glass walls. The view is magnificent.

But the most dramatic element is the roof, which seems to float on air.

It consists of nine steel "umbrellas," each supported on a single steel column, and sheathed with wood. In addition to avoiding any inside walls, this design provides a ten-foot overhang to shield the glass walls from sun and rain.

The three bedrooms and two baths, laundry, utility and storage

rooms, and the main entrance, are on a lower level cut into the hillside.

It's significant that the steel framing amounted to only seven per cent of the home's total cost!

These days architects are doing imaginative things with steel—and they do it economically.

Steel for Strength . . . Economy . . . Versatility

BETHLEHEM STEEL BETHLEHEM STEEL

Bethlehem Steel does not furnish plans for houses, but we would be happy to send you idea-provoking literature illustrating what architects are doing with steel framing from coast to coast. Write Publications Department, Room 1039B, Bethlehem Steel Company, Bethlehem, Pa.

Significant architects and master builders, natives of or associated with the Connecticut River Valley, who crafted historic houses of enduring beauty and interest, include Asher Benjamin, Thomas Hayden, Samuel Belcher, Jeremiah Gladwin, Isaac Damon, Chauncey Shepherd, Simon Sanborn, Henry Sykes, William Fenno Pratt, Ithiel Town and A.J. Davis, Henry Austin, Jabez Comstock, Lambert Packer, John Mead, Charles Platt, and the Norwich, Vermont, Mid-century modern architects Edgar and Margaret Hunter. House clients also commissioned New York– and Boston-based architects and landscape architects to design their homes in the valley. For clients Henry and Shavaun Towers, architect Ulrich Franzen designed a glass-walled box on an elevated site in Essex, Connecticut, that overlooked the Connecticut River and Long Island Sound. Constructed in 1957, the house featured an unusual steel frame of nine umbrella-like roof sections. The temple-like design was featured in this advertisement for Bethlehem Steel in *Sunset Magazine* in May 1961. (Francis Loeb Library, Harvard University.)

Seven

RIVER REFORMERS

Connecticut River Valley men and women usually took the lead in American reform movements. Steeped in religious righteousness, encouraged to participate in town governance, and well-educated, these men and women did not hesitate to share their opinions. They lobbied elected officials for the betterment of their society, but frequently faced stiff blowback due to entrenched beliefs, traditions, misogyny, and racism. Powerful elitists steadfastly favored the status quo.

The valley was a hotbed of religious fervor and home to experimental communities, including John Humphrey Noyes's Perfectionists (or Free-Lovers) of Putney, Vermont, and two Shaker communes. Valley folks were not immune to fringe ideas, which were promoted with zeal (and an eye on profits). Hydropathic "water-cure" establishments dotted the valley in the 19th century. Northampton, Massachusetts's, Sylvester Graham (whose cracker is better known) fostered strict hygiene regimens and vegetarianism, while Frank Fowler of East Haddam, Connecticut, in 1890, funded his mansion, one of the largest game preserves in the country, and a 110-foot yacht on the Connecticut River on proceeds from concocted remedies for male sexual dysfunction. Temperance, however, was always a mainstream movement.

While experiments in communal living and quack therapies were short-lived, reform-mindedness always burned bright. The most effective reformers were those dissatisfied with the oversights of the nation's founding fathers and the flaws of the country's founding principles. Slavery, unequal property and voting rights for freed blacks and women, lack of access to educational opportunity, poverty, homelessness, disease, harmful work conditions, and environmental degradation were all issues that these men and women faced head-on. The homes of Henry Barnard (built in 1807), a leading 19th-century advocate for education reform, and John James McCook (built in 1782), who investigated the causes of homelessness, both stand today on Hartford, Connecticut's, Main Street. US senator and farmer George Aiken (1892–1984) of Putney, Vermont, legislated to create programs to end hunger, establish minimum wages, and ensure civil rights.

Many valley reformers understood that their reform causes were related. They worked diligently for the abolition of slavery, poverty, and disease, and for universal suffrage, temperance, and educational advancement. Their homes remind us of the importance of their work—much unfinished.

The home of the five Smith sisters (above) in Glastonbury, Connecticut, is a national historic landmark because of its association with this extraordinarily well-educated, talented, theologically nonconforming, and reform-minded family. Abby and Julia Smith (left to right at left around 1877), along with their mother, polymath Hannah, and sister Hancy, were politically active in the reform causes of abolitionism, suffrage, education for all, and equal rights for women. They authored petitions, spoke at conventions and before Congress, and hosted antislavery meetings here. When abolitionist William Lloyd Garrison was banned from the local pulpits, he gave his speech standing on a tree stump in the front yard. Julia, also a classics scholar, was the first woman (and single person) to translate the Bible from its original languages; her translation was typeset and printed by women. (Above, CTSL; left, AM.)

ABBY SMITH AND HER COWS.

In a case that attracted national attention in 1873, Abby and Julia Smith refused to pay property tax, protesting that as unenfranchised women, they were unfairly taxed without representation. Their Alderney cows and 15 acres were seized by town authorities for nonpayment of taxes and only returned after the Smith sisters won their case in a protracted court battle, bringing attention to women's rights. Julia depicted Abby and her returned livestock (above) in her 1877 publication about the case. Known as the Kimberly Mansion for its original owner, the five-bay Colonial was purchased by father Zephaniah Smith in 1790. The Smiths' house lot stretched from Main Street to the Connecticut River (and still does). It is visible in the distance in the painting of her home (below) by Laurilla, another talented Smith sister. (Above, HGS; below, CTHS.)

The five communal families of Shakers of Enfield, Connecticut, were not just religious dissenters and celibates, but also ardent reformers. They were abolitionists harboring fugitive slaves, pacifists, isolationists, and feminists supporting women's suffrage. Between 1792 and 1917, their village grew to 100 buildings (15 of which are extant), including the North family dwelling also known as the Sisters' House" (above, at rear). Besides caring for the poor and indigent, Shakers welcomed curious tourists. Many of the communal dwellings included advanced technology for the period, such as steam heat, running water, and kitchen appliances. Shakers were self-reliant, hardworking, and entrepreneurial, selling many products such as packaged seeds, farm produce, and livestock, as well as manufacturing items such as woven rugs, pincushions, and baskets. A lasting legacy of the Shakers is their simple, utilitarian objects and furniture—designs considered protomodern by many, and frequently reproduced. (Both, CSHC.)

The Hill-Ross Farm (above) in Florence, a village of Northampton, Massachusetts, was the home of antislavery men Samuel Hill and Austin Ross—a documented stop on the Underground Railroad. Hill and others established the Northampton Association of Education and Industry, a utopian community of abolitionists that employed fugitive and free black men to produce thread from silkworms harvested from mulberry trees. The Hill-Ross Farm was the agricultural headquarters for the 478-acre community. Visitors included Sojourner Truth and David Ruggles, who went on to become important advocates for equal rights. Samuel Hill continued as a silk manufacturer, pictured at the door of his new house that he built nearby in 1845 (below). In a schoolhouse behind this house, Hill, a philanthropist committed to education for all, established in 1876 one of the first free kindergartens in the country. (Above, AM; below, FLib.)

Dwight Lyman Moody forever changed Northfield, Massachusetts, when he returned to his birthplace and childhood home (above around 1920) to found Northfield Seminary for Young Ladies (1879), and in 1881 the Mount Hermon School for Boys across the river in Gill. Moody was an evangelical preacher with an international following and a special interest in educating the poor and minorities. His work appealed to many religious denominations. Every summer, thousands came from across the country to attend Moody's Northfield Conferences on the Connecticut River. Moody transformed the quiet farming village into a Christian revival camp and later a fashionable resort. Moody and his wife, Emma, lived in a house on Main Street (below around 1885). It is thought that the elderly woman on the porch is Emma Moody. Her children play croquet with visiting cousins and a pet goat, a gift to Moody from the Holy Land. (Both, NMHA.)

Frank and Clara Churchill constructed their Queen Anne–style home (above in 1900), designed by Boston architect John Fox, in 1892 in Lebanon, New Hampshire. Churchill (inset above) visited nearly every state in the union as a traveling salesman for his company Carter & Churchill, manufacturers of clothing. A community banking and political leader in Lebanon, Churchill is best known as an advocate for Native Americans. From 1899 to 1909, he served the US Interior Department as a revenue inspector and special agent for Indian affairs. Churchill lobbied for taxation to fund free public schooling for children throughout the Oklahoma Territory and for native control of reindeer herds in Alaska. Clara, traveling with him, amassed an important collection of aboriginal artifacts. Seen below in 1921, Clara (at the organ) practices for a concert in her parlor, surrounded by her collections. (Both, LHS.)

The exceptionally well-detailed Federal-style house above was built by Abram Mitchell in Chester, Connecticut, in about 1820. The distinctive, operable oval window with the eagle at the center of its spider web pattern is a notable feature. Civil War surgeon Dr. Ambrose Pratt had occupied the Mitchell House from 1844, where he established the Chester Water-Cure and Medico-Surgical Infirmary, specializing in water-cure practices. Pratt advertised his resort as having a 20-acre farm with "a full two miles view of Connecticut River and its fine scenery" (below left around 1880). However, in 1866, the state medical establishment denounced him as a "quack and a pretender" for having abandoned the allopathic system for his hydropathic method. Pratt's daughter Ella Fitch took the photograph below right of her mother and sisters tending the gardens at their home around 1880. (All, ChHS.)

Isabella Beecher Hooker and John Hooker (below in 1897) were the original developers, with Francis Gillette, of Hartford, Connecticut's, Nook Farm neighborhood, which became one of the nation's most important literary colonies. They built the first house there in 1853 (above) in the Gothic Revival style; it was expanded by architect Octavius Jordan. John Hooker was a lawyer and abolitionist. Isabella was an ardent feminist, lecturer, and organizer of the women's suffrage movement in Connecticut. She testified often before Congress in favor of equal voting rights for women. In Hartford, she hosted national suffragist leaders Susan B. Anthony, Elizabeth Cady Stanton, and Victoria Woodhull. The Hookers drafted, and were instrumental in the passage of, a law that guaranteed Connecticut women equal property rights. (Above, HBSC; below, CTHS.)

The house adjacent to the riverfront landing at Hadlyme, Connecticut (above around 1959), was constructed by Henry Comstock, shipbuilder and manager of the ferry operation there, around 1805. Starting in 1916, it was the country home of the remarkable Hamilton sisters, pictured at left. From left to right are owners Margaret Hamilton and Alice Hamilton, Margaret's life partner Clara Landsberg, and unidentified. Alice was a physician, professor of pathology, and the first woman appointed to Harvard University's faculty. She was a research scientist, focusing on the occupational dangers of industrial chemicals (especially lead), a social-welfare reformer intensely interested in the health of American workers, pioneering in the field of industrial hygiene. Margaret was a teacher and headed Bryn Mawr School. Edith Hamilton, a sister, authored books on Greek and Roman mythology, while another sister, Norah Hamilton, was an accomplished artist. (Both, SLHRI.)

Famous actress Katharine Hepburn, a Hartford, Connecticut, native, lived in the Fenwick Borough of Old Saybrook, Connecticut, at the mouth of the Connecticut River overlooking Long Island Sound. After the 1938 hurricane destroyed her family's wood cottage, they rebuilt it in brick (above). Good-natured and intrepid Hepburn poses below among its wreckage. Her mother was Katharine Houghton Hepburn, a leading suffragette, advocate for birth control, and co-founder of Planned Parenthood. The actress played an important role in bringing attention to Connecticut River pollution. In 1965, she narrated *The Long Tidal River*, a documentary produced by brother-in-law Ellsworth Grant, in which she claimed the river was "the world's most beautifully landscaped cesspool." Her efforts led to Connecticut's Clean Water Bill of 1967, subsequent sewage treatment facilities, and the curbing of industrial and agricultural pollutants that had been dumped into the river's watershed for years. (Both, AM.)

Discover Thousands of Local History Books Featuring Millions of Vintage Images

Arcadia Publishing, the leading local history publisher in the United States, is committed to making history accessible and meaningful through publishing books that celebrate and preserve the heritage of America's people and places.

Find more books like this at
www.arcadiapublishing.com

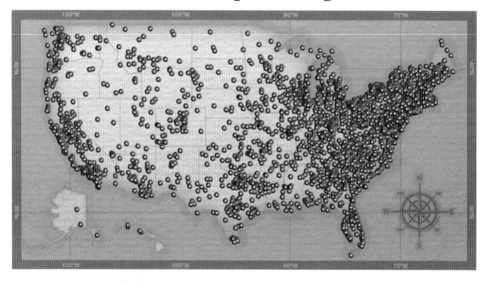

Search for your hometown history, your old stomping grounds, and even your favorite sports team.

Consistent with our mission to preserve history on a local level, this book was printed in South Carolina on American-made paper and manufactured entirely in the United States. Products carrying the accredited Forest Stewardship Council (FSC) label are printed on 100 percent FSC-certified paper.

MADE IN THE USA